D0816266

Meet the
Methodists

Meet the Methodists

An Introduction to The United Methodist Church

Revised Edition

Charles L. Allen

ABINGDON PRESS
Nashville

MEET THE METHODISTS
Copyright © 1986 by Abingdon Press.
Revised Edition © 1998 by Abingdon Press.

All rights reserved.
Study Guide © 1998 by Abingdon Press.

No part of this work may be reproduced or transmitted in any form or by any means, electronic or mechanical, including photocopying and recording, or by any information storage or retrieval system, except as may be expressly permitted by the 1976 Copyright Act or in writing from the publisher. Requests for permission should be addressed in writing to Abingdon Press, 201 Eighth Avenue South, Nashville, TN 37203.

This book is printed on acid-free paper.

Library of Congress Cataloging-in-Publication Data

Allen, Charles Livingstone, 1913-
  Meet the Methodists.
  1. Methodist Church. 2. United Methodist Church (U.S.)
I. Title. II. Title: United Methodist primer.
BX8331.2.A44   1986   287'.6   85-28794

ISBN 0-687-08232-3 (pbk.: alk. paper)

Scripture quotations unless otherwise noted are from the New Revised Standard Version of the Bible, copyrighted © 1989 by the Division of Christian Education of the National Council of the Churches of Christ in the United States of America, and are used by permission. All rights reserved.

98 99 00 01 02—15 14 13 12 11 10

MANUFACTURED IN THE UNITED STATES OF AMERICA

In memory of
the Reverend J. R. Allen, my father
and
Bishop Marvin A. Franklin, my uncle

CONTENTS

PREFACE

In writing these pages I was guided by previous *Primers* written by Bishop Charles Claude Selecman, Bishop Paul Washburn, and Bishop James Armstrong. Each of these editions was extremely well written and rendered great service to the church. From the previous editions I have both quoted and used ideas and thoughts.

From the foreword of *The John Wesley Reader,* compiled by Al Bryant (Word Books), I have used some material that I had earlier written for that volume.

The Book of Discipline of The United Methodist Church is a magnificent publication. I have used it frequently in writing these pages. I urge members of our church to obtain a *Discipline.* Reading it will be interesting, educational, and inspiring.

During this endeavor, I found myself re-reading with renewed interest notes I took in my church history classes at Candler School of Theology. My professor was William T. Watkins—a truly great teacher.

I express appreciation to Mrs. Mildred Parker for her assistance in preparing this manuscript.

In writing these pages my understanding and appreciation of my church has increased.

Charles L. Allen

1

THE CHURCH

The United Methodist Church is part of a tradition that has been an activity of human beings as far back in history as can be traced. As far as we can tell, all people who have ever lived on this earth have had some form of worship of God.

Human beings have, as a part of their very nature, an instinctive belief in a higher power. Nowhere in the Bible are we commanded to believe in God; that is taken for granted. People use different names for God, but all instinctively believe. In every society of which history knows, some people have worshiped together the higher power in which they believed. That practice has continued to this day.

People on the earth today hold several major religions—Buddhism, Hinduism, Islam, Judaism, and Christianity, as well as some others. The United Methodist Church is part of the stream of faith that includes Abraham, Moses, David, and the prophets. We, along with Judaism, hold the Old Testament to be the Word of God. But we believe that a major new beginning on this earth took place in the coming of Jesus Christ, as recorded in the New Testament. "For God so loved the world that he gave his only Son, so that everyone who believes in him may not perish but may have eternal life" (John 3:16).

Jesus Christ is the beginning of the Christian faith.

"He said to them, 'But who do you say that I am?' Simon Peter answered, 'You are the Messiah, the Son of the living God.' And Jesus answered him, 'Blessed are you, Simon son of Jonah! For flesh and blood has not revealed this to you, but my Father in heaven. And I tell you, you are Peter, and on this rock I will build my church, and the gates of Hades will not prevail against it' " (Matthew 16:15-18).

The United Methodist Church is part of the Christian faith and of the church that Jesus built on the foundation of belief in him, the Son of the living God. The beginnings of the church are recorded in the Book of Acts.

In 1517, Martin Luther nailed his ninety-five theses to the door of the church in Wittenburg, Germany, protesting against abuses in the Catholic Church. (Eventually his followers were called Lutherans.) Thus began what is known as the Protestant Reformation. In the same century, John Calvin broke with Catholicism, becoming the father of the Reformed tradition (including Presbyterianism); and King Henry VIII of England took over the headship of the church in his country, forming the Anglican Church (Church of England), known in its branches outside of England as the Episcopal Church. The United Methodist Church is part of the Protestant movement and traces its history back to the Anglican Church.

THE FIRST METHODIST SOCIETY

John Wesley, the founder of The Methodist Church, who was himself an Anglican priest, wrote the following account of the first society called Methodist:

"In November, 1729, four young gentlemen of Oxford—Mr. John Wesley, Fellow of Lincoln College; Mr. Charles Wesley, Student of Christ Church; Mr. Morgan, Commoner of Christ Church; and Mr. Kirkman, of Merton College—began...reading chiefly the Greek Testament. The next year, two or three of Mr. Wesley's pupils desired the liberty of meeting with them; and afterwards one of Mr. Charles Wesley's pupils. It was in 1732 that Mr. Ingham, of Queens's College, and Mr. Broughton, of Exeter, were added to their number. To these, in April, was joined Mr. Clayton of Brazen-nose, with two or three of his pupils. About the same time Mr. James Hervey was permitted to meet with them, and afterwards Mr. Whitefield."

This club was started by Charles Wesley during the second year of his student life at Oxford (1727). He persuaded two or three others to join with him in organizing a society. They met first every Sunday evening, then two evenings a week, and finally every evening from six until nine o'clock. Their meetings and deportment attracted the attention of both faculty and students. One of the students said, "Here is a new sect of Methodists sprung up."

John Wesley was not at Oxford when the society was first formed. When he returned, he immediately associated himself with the society and was recognized as its head. Their activities included the study of the Bible in Hebrew and Greek; the study of the classics; visits to the prison and the poor and the sick; and religious instruction of poor children. At the time the work of the society was so novel that the news of it spread beyond Oxford. They met with both praise and harsh criticism. The society was called by various names, such as Bible Moths, The Reformers' Club, The Godly Club, The Enthusiasts, and The Holy Club; but the name Methodists stuck. Though it was sometimes applied in derision, the Wesleys welcomed the term. Today millions of people in all parts of the world are happy to bear the name.

(Bishop Charles C. Selecman, *The Methodist Primer,* 1944)

WHY THE CHURCH?

Why is there such an organization as the church? Why does the church continue? Here are some answers to these questions:

(1) There is no such thing as a solitary religion. Religious faith is both love for God and love for people. The church provides for both expressions of love.

(2) The church is necessary to human nature. Human beings have strong urges toward both the self and the group. Persons have a social instinct that is frustrated if they do not work out their spiritual life in corporate fellowship. Private devotions and corporate communion with God are both necessary expressions of human beings.

(3) The church is the extension of the incarnation of God: "And the Word became flesh and lived among us" (John 1:14). Just as Christ is the incarnation of God, so the church is the incarnation of Christ—thus we speak of the church as "the body of Christ." The Christian church is a physical representative of Christ on this earth.

(4) The church is the best serving institution this world has ever known. Education for the masses was begun by the church, as were hospitals, children's homes, and charitable institutions too numerous to mention. Church people are people who care about other people.

(5) The church contains the best human life in the world. There are some exceptions both in and out of the church—but they *are* exceptions. The Christian faith offers people the motive and the power to change and transform their lives.

(6) The church is the one unbroken fellowship in the world. The *Epistle to Diognetus* was written at the time when the military might of the Roman Empire was falling to pieces. In that epistle we read, "What the soul is to the body, so the Christians are to the world— they hold the world together."

The words of Celsus, spoken in the second century, are just as true today, "The Christians love each other even before they are acquainted." Love for God and for one another—they go together.

(7) The church gives a sense of solidarity to all the centuries. The Bible was written for a people many years ago; yet it is no less applicable to the lives of people today. When Paul speaks of "we," he is referring to people of his day; his references, however, include all of us in this day as well. Today when Christians use the term "we," it includes not only us in the church but also our parents, grandparents, and even the first apostles. Likewise our "we" includes our children and even generations yet unborn. The church links all children of God into one unbroken stream. Jesus referred to this stream when he prayed, not only for his disciples, but for all who would believe through their word (John 17:20).

(8) The denomination is not the church. We United Methodists believe we are part of the family of Christians. Christians give allegiance to the church through a denomination.

(9) The church is not the kingdom of God. God brings God's kingdom. Christians pray, "Thy kingdom come." The purpose of the church is to help people enter God's kingdom. As part of God's kingdom, we serve humanity.

Once when I was driving in the country of Jordan, I stopped in a small community for lunch. Before getting back to my car, I saw about twenty school children coming down the street. They were happy, laughing children. Walking over to the children, I began talking with them; but there was an insurmountable language barrier. Then I held out my arms, and four of the little children came to me smiling. There with them I realized that all children belong to God.

(10) We believe in eternal life. The church is the most effective voice on earth that assures us of the fact of eternal life.

THE HOLY CATHOLIC CHURCH

The Apostles' Creed is a confession of faith for many Christian churches. In the Apostles' Creed, United Methodist churches join with many other churches in confessing their faith in "the holy catholic church." Those words do not refer to the Roman Catholic Church; they mean that beyond our loyalty to our own denomination, we believe in the church universal.

2

THE UNITED METHODIST CHURCH

The United Methodist Church began with John Wesley. To understand the church it is necessary to know about him. He was born in Epworth, England, June 17, 1703. He died in London, March 2, 1791. Those eighty-eight years contained a most remarkable life.

Wesley's first ten years were spent in the parsonage in Epworth, in Norfolk County, where his father, the Reverend Samuel Wesley, a minister in the Church of England, was rector. Perhaps no experience affected Wesley's life more than the one that occurred on February 9, 1709, when he was not quite six years old. The family home was on fire. It was thought that all the family were safely out of the house. Then it was discovered that John was trapped in an upstairs room. He was rescued, and on the very spot—as the house was burning—his mother dedicated the child to God anew, saying he was "a brand plucked out of the burning."

John Wesley was no self-made man. He attended Charterhouse and Oxford University. Those were two of the finest schools in all the world. There, his acute mind and sensitive soul were greatly influenced by a thorough formal education. His father, grandfather, and great-grandfather had been Oxford men before him; and he was proud to be in the Oxford tradition. He gained a reputation for scholarship and became an intellectually outstanding man.

For nine years Wesley served as a fellow of Lincoln College, with a brief interim as his father's assistant in the capacity of parish clergyman. Later he came to Savannah, Georgia, as a missionary; and here we see the beginning of the breakdown of Wesley's high-church religion. His ministry in Georgia was not successful. He wrote in his journal, "Why (what was least of all expected), that I, who went to

America to convert others, was never myself converted to God," though later he wrote in the margin, "I doubt this."

In Savannah, Wesley came to know a Moravian pastor by the name of August Spangenberg. On the ship coming to Georgia, Wesley had found himself cringing with fear in the midst of a storm; but the Moravians on board faced the peril with perfect poise. The fact that they were different from himself broke Wesley's pride. Upon his return to England, he came to know an outstanding Moravian, Peter Bohler, who had come there from Frankfurt, Germany.

ALDERSGATE

The story here must be told in Wesley's own words:

> In the evening I went very unwillingly to a society in Aldersgate Street, where one was reading Luther's preface to the *Epistle to the Romans*. About a quarter before nine, while he was describing the change which God works in the heart through faith in Christ, I felt my heart strangely warmed. I felt I did trust in Christ, Christ alone for salvation; and an assurance was given me that He had taken away *my* sins, even *mine*, and saved *me* from the law of sin and death.
>
> I began to pray with all my might for those who had in a more especial manner despitefully used me and persecuted me. I then testified openly to all there what I now first felt in my heart.

This was on Wednesday evening, May 24, 1738. That was the rising of the sun in John Wesley's life—the sun that never set.

Today as we look back on the eighteenth century, we see three great movements: the rise of the Anglo-Saxon nations (specifically the expansion of the British Empire and the rise of the United States), the rise of Methodism, and the rise of the great modern missionary movement. John Wesley might say of all of them, *Quorem pars magna fui* (Of which things I was an important part). These three were believed to converge upon a common object—the salvation of humankind. Wesley expressed this view in saying, "The world is my parish." Each of these three movements would have suffered without the support of the others.

FOUR MOMENTOUS DECISIONS

During the year following his Aldersgate experience, John Wesley made four momentous decisions, which eventually led to the founding and worldwide mission of The Methodist Church: *First, he approved field preaching.* Wesley found himself shut out of the churches because of the content of his preaching, so he took to the open fields. His high-church scruples against preaching anywhere but in a pulpit were melted away by the opportunities of evangelism. This was the forerunner of revivalism.

Second, he approved of lay preaching. It would have been utterly impossible to get ordained ministers to carry on this new movement. People were being converted and needed biblical teaching. To permit the unordained to preach was scandalous to high-church officials, but John Wesley stood by that decision.

Third, Wesley decided to organize converts and to give them some kind of supervision. He became a practical churchman.

Fourth, Wesley decided to house his societies. The actual beginning of the world's first Methodist chapel was at Bristol, May 12, 1739. Later a chapel was built in London—the Foundry—and soon a second chapel was built in London. From such beginnings, the housing of Methodism went on.

Was Wesley conscious of the significance of what he was doing? The answer is no. Like Abraham, the father of the faithful, he rose at the call of God and went out, knowing not whither. Those who are dedicated to God never worry about what the results will be. This brings to mind such notables as Moses at the burning bush, Paul on the road to Damascus, and men like Martin Luther and John Calvin and John Knox. Like them, Wesley became a hero of the faith.

John Wesley never professed to discover new truths; he was concerned to restore the old faith. He was no innovator but a renovator. As one reads the excellent collection of readings from John Wesley's sermons and journals, two errors concerning John Wesley and Methodism are completely dispelled. Some have thought that Wesley cared nothing for doctrinal truth and that he made Methodism a movement of doctrineless sentiment and creedless enthusiasm. Others have imagined that Wesley preached new doctrines never known to the church before his time and that Methodism came from this new teaching. Both of these ideas are completely in error. Wesley's preaching and teaching were based on the teaching of Scripture.

DOCTRINES WESLEY PREACHED

Here let us sum up briefly the doctrines that John Wesley preached:

(1) the doctrine of the authority and inspiration of the Holy Scriptures.

(2) the doctrine of the depravity of human nature and inability of persons to turn to God without the aid of the Holy Spirit.

(3) the doctrine of the atonement of Christ, made through his vicarious sacrifice for the sin of the world, which is the sole meritorious cause for human acceptance with God.

(4) the doctrine of the universality of that atonement, whereby "whoever believes...shall not perish but have eternal life."

(5) the doctrine of justification by faith alone as the instrumental cause of a person's salvation.

(6) the doctrine of new birth and the absolute need of a conscious conversion or regeneration.

(7) the doctrine of sanctification by the cleansing power of the Holy Ghost through faith in Christ.

(8) the doctrine of the witness of the Spirit, bearing witness with the spirit of a regenerated person that he or she is a child of God.

John Wesley met the needs of his day and generation, with its masses of people who were defeated. He declared the availability of God's grace for all people—that every person is a child of God. To the churches he proclaimed a salvation that would make religion a power instead of a burden, that would lift religion from drudgery to joyful fellowship with God. The gospel that John Wesley preached was "good news" to the people of his day. His translation of Christ and his message into terms that promised people of his time salvation literally transformed a century.

One thing further—John Wesley was concerned with the society in which he lived. For him religion was not merely an emotional experience; it was a program of action that called for a plan of attack wherever an evil was damaging the lives of people. He especially waged his fight against what he regarded as the four greatest evils of his age: poverty, war, ignorance, and disease. After more than a half century of war against these evils, one can say that the modern social conscience had been born.

Wesley believed that each person is a "steward" of wealth, not an owner. It has been claimed that Wesley was the founder of modern philanthropy and that his attitude toward human need was far in advance of the older attitude of almsgiving charity.

Wesley was an untiring enemy of ignorance. It was his theory that every person is entitled to the blessing of education. It may be that his theories of education were lacking at some points, but his conviction as to who should be educated gives him a place in the history of education. Green, the historian, states, "Wesley gave the first impulse to our popular education."

Wesley was not a pacifist in the modern sense, but he believed passionately that people of reason ought to be able to settle their differences. To Wesley's mind, war was insanity. He felt there was no need to discuss war in relation to religion. War stood condemned on the basis of "common sense."

Wesley was deeply concerned with human suffering. In London he organized a group of volunteers who systematically visited the sick. London was divided into twenty-three sections, with two visitors assigned to each section. They were instructed not only to inquire into the spiritual state of the sick but also to discover their trouble and to seek medical advice, to relieve them if they were in want, and to render any other needed service. John Wesley believed in a practical application of Christianity. (These principles are discussed more fully in Chapter 6 of this book.)

THE WESLEY FAMILY

John Wesley was the son of Samuel Wesley, the grandson of John Wesley, and the great grandson of Bartholomew Wesley, all three of whom were graduates of Oxford University.

John Wesley's mother was Susanna Annesley Wesley, the daughter of Dr. Samuel Annesley, an English clergyman. She received an excellent education and became a wonderful teacher. Susanna taught each of her many children to read at the age of five, and all were educated at home. She was extremely thorough as a teacher and gave to all her children, including John, a wonderful educational and spiritual background.

John's most famous brother was Charles, who was four years younger. Charles wrote the hymns for the early Methodists—many of which are now in *The United Methodist Hymnal.* Among his best-loved hymns are "Jesus, Lover of My Soul," "Love Divine, All Loves Excelling," "A Charge to Keep I Have," "O for a Thousand Tongues to Sing," and "Hark, the Herald Angels Sing." It is said that Charles Wesley wrote over six thousand hymns.

A CHURCH BEGINS

John Wesley did not plan to found a new church. He felt God had called him to preach the gospel of Jesus Christ as an ordained minister in the Church of England and to minister to those whom he won to the Christian life. To do so, he gathered the new converts in groups, classes, and societies, and appointed lay people as leaders. He encouraged those whom he had chosen to preach to the people on the streets, in homes, and wherever there was opportunity. Once a year he called these leaders together for a conference. Only after Wesley's death did the new leaders of Wesley's societies decide to leave the Church of England and to become The Methodist Church.

Wesley emphasized three important activities:

(1) *Evangelism*—"The world is my parish," he said over and over. He did not wait for the people to come to him or to the meetings. He preached and practiced going out to find the people.

(2) *Organization and administration*—In this way the fruits of evangelism were conserved and extended.

(3) *Education*—He believed in teaching and learning. The printed page was most important in Wesley's life.

THE UNITED SOCIETY

The opposition by the established church to Wesley's preaching and the persecution of new Christians only intensified the zeal of the Methodists and served to spread the news of their work throughout England.

Naturally the followers of Wesley, having received new faith and hope, would come together to exchange their experiences and to talk of their new relation to God. This gave rise to the organization of [Methodist] societies in London, Bristol, and other towns and villages. Methodist chapels were also built. The cornerstone of the first Methodist chapel was laid in Bristol, May 12, 1739.

Wesley was a genius in organization. He proposed to form these societies into a United Society. His account of the formation of the United Society is as follows:

"In the latter end of the year 1739 eight or ten persons who appeared to be deeply convicted of sin, and earnestly groaning for redemption, came to Mr. Wesley in London. They desired, as did two or three more the next day, that he would spend some time with them in prayer, and advise them how to flee from the wrath to come, which they saw continually hanging over their heads. That he might have more time for this great work, he appointed a day when they all might come together; which from thenceforward they did every week, namely on Thursday, in the evening. To these, and as many more as desired to join with them (for their number increased daily), he gave advices from time to time which he judged most needful for them; and they always concluded their meetings with prayer suited to their several necessities.

"This was the rise of the United Society, first in Europe, and then in America. Such a society is not other than a company of [people] having the form and seeking the power of godliness, united in order to pray together, to receive the word of exhortation, and to watch over one another in love, that they may help each other to work out their salvation."

There was only one condition previously required of those who desired membership in the Society, namely:

A desire to flee from the wrath to come, and to be saved from their sins.

Those who desired to continue in the Society, however, were expected to evidence their desire for salvation:

"First: by doing no harm, avoiding evil in every kind, especially that which is most generally practiced; such as, taking the name of God in vain, profaning the day of the Lord, drunkenness, buying or selling spirituous liquors, fighting, quarreling, brother going to law with brother, breaking the Golden Rule, softness, making bad debts, borrowing or buying with the probability of not paying.

"Second: by doing good of every possible sort, and, as far as possible, to all [people].

"Third: by attending upon all the ordinances of God."

(See *The Book of Discipline*, General Rules)

These simple General Rules signify the high moral standards set for early Methodists. The Methodist movement was more than a wave of religious enthusiasm. It demanded a pure motive, a joyful experience, and a blameless life.

They were not required to accept or affirm a creed. To this day conduct rather than creed is the test of membership in [The United Methodist] Church.

(Selecman, *The Methodist Primer,* pages 16-18)

METHODISM GOES ABROAD

Methodism spread first to Ireland and then to America. In 1760 Philip Embury, a lay preacher from Ireland, came to New York City. About the same time another lay preacher from Ireland, Robert Strawbridge, came to Frederick County, Maryland. In 1769 Wesley sent Richard Boardman and Joseph Pilmore to America. In 1771, Francis Asbury came to America. He became the leader of American Methodism.

Within ten years after the first Methodist preachers arrived, American Methodism numbered about fifteen thousand members and eighty preachers. There was need for these preachers to become ordained, and Wesley requested ordination from the Bishop of London; but he refused. So Wesley himself ordained two men and appointed Dr. Thomas Coke, a presbyter in the Church of England, as a general superintendent "to preside over the flock of Christ in America." Wesley directed Coke to ordain Francis Asbury as a super-intendent.

On December 24, 1784, about sixty preachers gathered at the Christmas Conference in Lovely Lane Chapel in Baltimore, Maryland, and organized the Methodist Episcopal Church in America. Coke and Wesley had sent to America *The Sunday Service,* which was a briefer form of the English *Book of Common Prayer.* Twenty-four of the thirty-nine Articles of Religion of the Church of England were adopted by the Methodists. One article of religion was added, recognizing the independence of the new nation. These arti-cles of religion are in the United Methodist *Book of Discipline.* Briefly they can be summarized as follows:

1. There is one true God, who has all power, wisdom, and good-ness. He made and preserves all things. Father, Son, and Holy Spirit are one God, the Trinity.

2. Jesus, the divine Son of God, was born of the virgin Mary, was crucified, died, and was buried for the sins of men.

3. Jesus Christ rose from the dead and ascended into heaven and will return at the last day to judge all men.

4. The Holy Spirit came from the Father and the Son and is one with them in the Trinity.

5. The Holy Scriptures (Old and New Testaments) contain all truth necessary for salvation.

6. The ancient rites and ceremonies of the Old Testament are not binding on Christians, but its moral teachings should be obeyed.

7. Original sin is the evil in human nature that we inherit.

8. The free will of man must have divine help in order that we may do good and please God.

9. We are justified, or pardoned, not by good works, but by faith in our Lord and Savior Jesus Christ.

10. Good works are the fruits of faith and are pleasing to God.

11. It is not possible to do more good works than God requires.

12. If we sin after we are justified, or pardoned, we may repent and be forgiven.

13. The church of Christ is a congregation of faithful Christians in which the gospel is preached and the sacraments are administered.

14. Purgatory is not taught in the Bible; neither is praying to saints or worshiping images or relics.

15. Public worship should not be conducted in a language that the people do not understand. To do so is contrary to the Word of God and the custom of the early Christian church.

16. Sacraments are badges or tokens of Christian profession and are signs of God's grace to us. Christ ordained only two sacraments: baptism and the Supper of the Lord.

17. Baptism is a sign of Christian profession. The baptism of young children should be retained in the church.

18. The sacrament of the Lord's Supper is a sign of Christian love and also a memorial of Christ's death. It should be observed in a spiritual manner but should not be made an object of worship.

19. In the Lord's Supper lay members should receive both bread and wine.

20. Christ's death is the only offering needed for sin. There is no value in masses for the dead. This is a dangerous deceit.

21. Ministers may marry at their own discretion.

22. It is not necessary to have the same rites and ceremonies in all places. These may be changed to meet the needs of different countries and times.

23. This article states the authority and independence of our national government.

24. Christians may possess private property, but they should give liberally to the poor.

25. A Christian may swear, when a magistrate requires it, without violating the teachings of the Bible.

DIVISIONS IN AMERICAN METHODISM

In 1828–30, there was an argument among Methodists over lay representation in the church. One group pulled out to become The Methodist Protestant Church.

In 1844, another division occurred. This time two issues were involved—the question of slavery and the constitutional issue over the powers of the General Conference versus the episcopacy. Both North and South kept the name Methodist Episcopal Church—the southern church merely added "South" after the name. On May 10, 1939, The Methodist Episcopal Church, The Methodist Episcopal Church, South, and The Methodist Protestant Church united to form The Methodist Church.

In 1946, The Church of the United Brethren in Christ and The Evangelical Church united to become The Evangelical United Brethren Church. Both groups began with German-speaking Christians in the Northeast and Midwest in the early 1800's, and their first leaders had ties with the Methodists. Philip Otterbein, the founder of the United Brethren in Christ, was a friend of Francis Asbury and took part in his ordination service. Jacob Albright, a leader in the early Evangelical Association, was a German-speaking farmer in Pennsylvania who became a Methodist preacher before beginning the Association in 1803. (See page 32.) The basic beliefs and practices of both traditions were similar to those of Methodism; and in 1968, The Methodist Church and The Evangelical United Brethren Church united to form The United Methodist Church.

The United Methodist Church embodies the history and tradition of the following churches that are Methodist in name and tradition:

The Methodist Episcopal Church
The Methodist Episcopal Church, South
The Methodist Protestant Church
The Methodist Church (merged into the Protestant Methodist
   Church in 1877)
United Brethren in Christ
The Evangelical Association
The United Evangelical Church
The Evangelical Church
The Methodist Church
The Evangelical United Brethren Church

1996 Statistical Review of The United Methodist Church*

In the Jurisdictional Conferences

Total lay members at end of 1994	8,549,007
Received on profession of faith	196,481
Received from other United Methodist churches	131,589
Received from other denominations	83,670
Removed or withdrawn	184,965
Removed by transfer to other UM churches	103,896
Removed by transfer to other denominations	48,421
Removed by death	123,060
Total lay members at end of 1995	8,500,405
Total itinerant members	38,403
Total full members	8,538,808

In the Central Conferences**

Total lay members	1,104,122
Total ordained members	3,232
Total full members	1,107,354
Total lay and ordained full members	9,646,162

*Source: *1996 General Minutes of the Annual Conferences of The United Methodist Church.* (Evanston, IL: The General Council on Finance and Administration, 1996), page 29.

**Central Conferences are those United Methodist conferences outside the United States. They are currently the fastest-growing conferences in The United Methodist Church.

Membership in The United Methodist Church Lay and Ministerial for 1995*

Jurisdiction	Total Full Members	Total Preparatory Members	Itinerant Ministers	Under Appointment	Total Annual Conference Ministerial Membership
North Central	1,691,136	333,596	9,240	386	9,626
Northeastern	1,651,638	303,757	7,712	318	8,030
South Central	1,815,987	285,148	6,898	368	7,266
Southeastern	2,887,718	357,054	11,225	546	11,771
Western	466,529	87,226	3,328	67	3,395
Military Service	4,021	2,943			
Totals	8,538,808	1,369,724	38,403	1,685	40,088

*Source: 1996 General Minutes, pages 71, 73.

3

METHODISM IN AMERICA

THE METHODIST EPISCOPAL CHURCH

The first annual conference in American Methodism convened in St. George's Church, Philadelphia, July 14, 1773, drawing delegates from three colonies.

In the back country of Maryland, Robert Strawbridge had invited his neighbors for worship in his log house on Sam's Creek. As people were converted and more churches formed, the Baltimore circuit was established, which reported to the Conference of 1773 thirty societies and five hundred members.

In October of 1766, Philip Embury preached to five persons in the living room of his rented house in New York. Soon the group outgrew the living room. On October 30, 1768, Embury preached the dedicatory sermon in John Street Church, believed by many to be the first Methodist church built in America.

In 1767, Captain Thomas Webb enrolled the first Methodists in Philadelphia and led them into St. George's Church. Thus Methodism in America began in the wooded hills of Frederick County, Maryland; in the small but growing port of New York; and in Philadelphia, the largest American city at that time.

Francis Asbury arrived in America from England in 1771 and immediately protested that there was insufficient "circulation of preachers." He felt that the preachers were inclined to stay in the cities rather than to go out into the rural areas. By the time of the Conference in 1773, Methodist preachers had driven stakes as far as Boston to the north and Norfolk and Petersburg, Virginia, to the south. However, in 1773, it is estimated there was only one Methodist among each 2,050 of America's population.

Eleven years later, the historic Christmas Conference convened in Lovely Lane Chapel, Baltimore. By 1784, America had greatly expanded to the south and west. From the Conference in 1773, ten Methodist preachers rode away from Philadelphia to their appointments, seeking to keep pace with those early American pioneers. Between 1773 and 1784, the number of circuits increased from 6 to 46; the number of preachers from 10 to 83; and the number of members from 1,160 to 14,988. Instead of one in every 2,050 persons in America being a Methodist, the ratio had decreased by 1784 to one in every 213.

The Christmas Conference gave the church a name, appointed Thomas Coke and Francis Asbury to places of administrative responsibility, and invested its ministers with an office that would command legal recognition and public respect.

Francis Asbury became the leader of American Methodism. He was a genius at planning, and he had that amazing personality that caused his associates quickly to turn to him for leadership. We Methodists today need to remember the names of some of those early preachers: mighty evangelists like Edward Dromgoole, John Easter, and John Tunnell; scholarly preachers like William Gill, John Dickens, and William Phoebus; pathfinders like John Smith, John Major, and Jeremiah Lambert; aggressive spirits like Jesse Lee, Freeborn Garrettson, Thomas Ware, Philip Bruce, and Nelson Reed. These preachers not only penetrated frontiers and formed new churches and circuits, they were ecclesiastical architects who laid lasting foundations.

When Asbury rode to his first American preaching place, America was on horseback. When he died forty-five years later, March 31, 1816, America was on wheels. Less than a quarter of a century later, Jason Lee preached in Oregon country. From the Atlantic coast to the Pacific coast was a long way—those wheels were wagon wheels—but Methodism made the journey. As Americans moved in every direction, Methodist preachers were there to hold revivals and to start churches.

In 1786, Thomas Humphries and John Major crossed the river from South Carolina into Wilkes County, Georgia. Near the place where the first Methodist church in Georgia was started now stands Smyrna United Methodist Church, which meets in a lovely white wooden building. (I remember, as a six-year-old boy, walking down the aisle in that church and making my public profession of faith in Christ. I remember my father, J. R. Allen, who was the pastor, raising money for the monument to the first Methodist church on Georgia soil and dedicating it. That monument stands there today.) In 1788, Asbury arrived there to meet with ten preachers in the first conference ever held in Georgia.

Jesse Lee once said, "Methodism can live wherever men can live." It was proved to be so as Methodism encountered hostile Native Americans in Alabama and Mississippi but constantly went on farther. It is a thrilling story, how Methodism advanced through the Cumberland Gap into Kentucky and Tennessee, where settlers from North Carolina and Virginia were expanding American horizons.

After the Revolutionary War, Methodism began to enter New England, where both the physical and the cultural climates were very different from those in the Middle Atlantic and southern states. Instead of a frontier life with all its hardships and violence, New England was a land of settled and steady habits. Theology was the issue here, not evangelism. Jesse Lee, a warmhearted Virginian, led the way through the cold, ecclesiastical atmosphere northward into Boston and Maine and from the coast into regions beyond the Green Mountains of Vermont.

In the 1780's, Methodism traveled west from Pennsylvania. The first Methodist sermon preached in Ohio was by George Callahan in 1787. By 1816, the year Asbury died, there were 18,150 Methodists in Ohio, a little less than one-third the entire membership of American Methodism. Methodism was also growing in Indiana and Illinois as those states increased their population. In 1804, Nathan Bangs set out from New York City for Detroit, a remote trading post. However, his preaching was not met with enthusiasm. Later, others came into that area with more success.

By 1816, the country beyond the Mississippi River was welcoming the Methodist preachers, and eight circuits were formed in Missouri along two hundred miles of the Mississippi. It is thought that the first Methodist sermon preached in Arkansas was by William Patterson, a Kentuckian, who settled in Helena about 1800.

By the time of Asbury's death, in 1816, Methodism had increased from 10 preachers and 1,160 members in 1773 to 695 preachers and 214,235 members. That was a remarkable gain. Now Methodists numbered one in every 39 Americans. From just five communities in five eastern colonies, Methodism was now established in every state and territory east of the Mississippi except eastern Florida, which was under the control of the Spanish, and Wisconsin, which had not yet had many second-generation American settlers (most were first-generation European immigrants).

In 1845, Texas was annexed; and within two or three years, the great area from New Mexico and Colorado westward—an area which now embraces half a dozen states—became open for settlement. Soon after news spread that gold was to be found in California, the covered wagons headed west in great numbers. The Native Americans bitterly opposed the spread of white settlers, and much fighting was done. However, Christian people in America sent missionaries into the Wild West to evangelize the Native Americans with much success. In 1832, the General Conference at Philadelphia constituted a Committee on Missions; and many itinerant preachers and teachers enlisted to go to our western and northwestern frontiers. They heeded the command: "Say among the heathen that the LORD reigneth" (Psalm 96:10, KJV).

By 1833, the first settlements were being made in Iowa, and during the next decade Methodism crossed Iowa and began building churches in Nebraska. The Plan of Separation of 1844, which divided the church into northern and southern factions, set Methodism back for a time in border areas such as Kansas, but not for long. By 1859, J. L. Dyer ("the Snowshoe Itinerant"), William H. Goode, Jerome C. Berryman, L. B. Stateler, and others were in Colorado and organized the Denver City and Auria Mission with 22 members. Methodism was carried into the Dakotas from Iowa about 1860. In 1872, the Rocky Mountain Conference was organized; and that same year W. W. Van Orsdel ("Brother Van") began preaching across Montana. By 1865, Methodist preachers were in Utah and Wyoming.

The Oregon and California Mission Conference of The Methodist Episcopal Church was organized in 1848; and in 1853, the California Conference was organized. From these conferences Methodism came back east into Idaho, Nevada, and Arizona.

In 1890, America was linked from the Atlantic coast to the Pacific with a solid band of states; but years before this happened, the oceans were connected by Methodist conferences across our land.

Evangelistic passion was what built the church in America—in homes, under brush arbors, in tabernacles, in frontier churches. Wherever people could be gathered together, the gospel was preached and the invitation was given. Evangelism may not have been the only business of early Methodism, but evangelism was the main business of early Methodism.

THE UNITED BRETHREN CHURCH

In 1767, Philip Otterbein, a university graduate and minister of a German Evangelical Reformed church in Baltimore, visited a group of Mennonites in Lancaster County, Pennsylvania, and heard a

Mennonite farmer, Martin Boehm, preach. After the service
Otterbein greeted Boehm with the words, *"Wir sind Bruder"* (We are
brothers"). Influenced by German pietism, Otterbein was a friend
of Francis Asbury. Boehm had studied Wesley's works and eventually joined The Methodist Episcopal Church. In 1800, fourteen
German ministers, including Boehm and Otterbein, met in the
home of Peter Kemp, near Frederick, Maryland, beginning the
practice of annual conferences; from that meeting the United
Brethren Church dates its beginning. In 1815, the group formally
organized, adopting a discipline very similar to the Methodist *Book
of Discipline.*

The church expanded westward in the following decades, first to
Ohio, then to Indiana. Total membership grew from 10,000 in 1813,
to 47,000 in 1850, and 61,000 in 1857. German immigrants
increased the size of the church, but it had English-speaking members also. Thus two sets of minutes were kept at many conferences,
and the *Discipline* was published in both English and German editions. They started a missionary society in 1841, established a seminary in 1871, and formed a Women's Missionary Association in
1875. The church split in 1889 over the issue of lay delegates to
General Conference and some other items; but by the turn of the
century there were more than 240,000 United Brethren, and by
1920 more than 340,000. In 1946, it joined with the Evangelical
Church to form The Evangelical United Brethren Church.

THE EVANGELICAL ASSOCIATION

Jacob Albright was a Lutheran farmer in Lancaster County,
Pennsylvania, in the late 1700's. After the death of three of his children, he was converted through the preaching of a Methodist local
preacher. He began to study Wesley's writings and joined a
Methodist class meeting. He started preaching in 1796, organizing
a number of new classes. In November 1803, the leaders of the
classes met and formed the Society of Evangelical Friends, with
Albright as the leader. They started annual conferences in 1807,
when the group reported membership of over 200. Leaders included John Walter, George Miller, Jacob Fry, and John Dreisbach.
Albright was made a bishop. They also voted to create a discipline,
based on the Methodist *Discipline.*

At the first General Conference in 1816, the group chose the
name Evangelical Association. By 1827, there was a Western
Conference for work in Ohio; and by 1837, Evangelicals had moved

to the Chicago area. The General Conference of 1836 authorized the establishment of a missionary society. Later leaders included John Seybert and William Orwig. By 1900 there were 166,000 Evangelicals. The church split in 1894, primarily over the use of the German language, but also over other issues. The two groups, the United Evangelical Church and the Evangelical Association, rejoined in 1922, forming the Evangelical Church. When the Evangelical Church joined with the United Brethren to form The Evangelical United Brethren Church in November, 1946, the new denomination had more than 700,000 members.

4

WHAT UNITED METHODISTS BELIEVE

Methodism from the beginning has been more life-centered than belief-centered. Yet, though Methodism has emphasized the warm heart, John Wesley was a man of scholarship who believed in education. The church he founded has emphasized from the beginning the value of a trained mind. No other Protestant church has done more to further the cause of education.

The twenty-five Articles of Religion (paraphrased in Chapter 2 of this book) are foundational beliefs of Methodist people.

The Apostles' Creed, which has come down from the early church (perhaps even as early as the second century, though its present form dates from about the seventh century), has always had a prominent place in Methodism. Today a great majority of Methodist congregations repeat this creed every Sunday.

THE APOSTLES' CREED

I believe in God the Father Almighty, maker of heaven and earth;

And in Jesus Christ his only Son our Lord: who was conceived by the Holy Spirit, born of the Virgin Mary, suffered under Pontius Pilate, was crucified, dead, and buried; the third day he rose from the dead; he ascended into heaven, and sitteth at the right hand of God the Father Almighty; from thence he shall come to judge the quick and the dead.

I believe in the Holy Spirit, the holy catholic church, the communion of saints, the forgiveness of sins, the resurrection of the body, and the life everlasting. Amen.

The Apostles' Creed affirms seven beliefs of Christian people:
1. God the Father
2. Jesus Christ his only Son
3. The Holy Spirit
4. The church
5. Forgiveness of sins
6. The Resurrection
7. Life everlasting

There are many other affirmations of faith printed in *The United Methodist Hymnal* (see the section, "Affirmations of Faith," beginning at 880). The three affirmations printed below have been used in Methodist services for at least sixty years. To carefully read the words of these creeds is inspiring.

THE NICENE CREED

We believe in one God, the Father, the Almighty, maker of heaven and earth, of all that is, seen and unseen.

We believe in one Lord, Jesus Christ, the only Son of God, eternally begotten of the Father, God from God, Light from Light, true God from true God, begotten, not made, of one Being with the Father; through him all things were made.
For us and for our salvation he came down from heaven, was incarnate of the Holy Spirit and the Virgin Mary and became truly human. For our sake he was crucified under Pontius Pilate; he suffered death and was buried. On the third day he rose again in accordance with the Scriptures; he ascended into heaven and is seated at the right hand of the Father. He will come again in glory to judge the living and the dead, and his kingdom will have no end.

We believe in the Holy Spirit, the Lord, the giver of life, who proceeds from the Father and the Son, who with the Father and the Son is worshiped and glorified, who has spoken through the prophets.
We believe in the one holy catholic and apostolic church.
We acknowledge one baptism for the forgiveness of sins.
We look for the resurrection of the dead, and the life of the world to come. Amen.

A MODERN AFFIRMATION

We believe in God the Father, infinite in wisdom, power, and love, whose mercy is over all his works, and whose will is ever directed to his children's good.

We believe in Jesus Christ, Son of God and Son of man, the gift of the Father's unfailing grace, the ground of our hope, and the promise of our deliverance from sin and death.

We believe in the Holy Spirit as the divine presence in our lives, whereby we are kept in perpetual remembrance of the truth of Christ, and find strength and help in time of need.

We believe that this faith should manifest itself in the service of love as set forth in the example of our blessed Lord, to the end that the kingdom of God may come upon the earth. Amen.

THE KOREAN CREED

We believe in the one God, creator and sustainer of all things, Father of all nations, the source of all goodness and beauty, all truth and love.

We believe in Jesus Christ, God manifest in the flesh, our teacher, example, and Redeemer, the Savior of the world.

We believe in the Holy Spirit, God present with us for guidance, for comfort, and for strength.

We believe in the forgiveness of sins, in the life of love and prayer, and in grace equal to every need.

We believe in the Word of God contained in the Old and New Testaments as the sufficient rule both of faith and of practice.

We believe in the church, those who are united in the living Lord for the purpose of worship and service.

We believe in the reign of God as the divine will realized in human society, and in the family of God, where we are all brothers and sisters.

We believe in the final triumph of righteousness and in the life everlasting. Amen.

THE BAPTISMAL COVENANT

Persons who are baptized and received into membership in The United Methodist Church are required to affirm their faith by answering yes to the following questions:

On behalf of the whole church, I ask you: Do you renounce the spiritual forces of wickedness, reject the evil powers of this world, and repent of your sin?

Do you accept the freedom and power God gives you to resist evil, injustice, and oppression in whatever forms they present themselves?

Do you confess Jesus Christ as your Savior, put your whole trust in his grace, and promise to serve him as your Lord, in union with the church which Christ has opened to people of all ages, nations, and races?

According to the grace given to you, will you remain a faithful member of Christ's holy church and serve as Christ's representative in the world?

As a member of Christ's universal church, will you be loyal to The United Methodist Church, and do all in your power to strengthen its ministries?

As a member of this congregation, will you faithfully participate in its ministries by your prayers, your presence, your gifts, and your service?

(*The United Methodist Hymnal,* pages 34 and 38)

BASIC BELIEFS AND DOCTRINES OF METHODISM

It is easily seen that in order to become a member of The United Methodist Church, one does not have to subscribe to a long list of beliefs. However, the church does have a very firm and clearly stated set of beliefs. The more prominent Methodist beliefs may be briefly stated as follows:

1. *The Bible.* The Bible is the inspired and holy Word of God. The Bible is our textbook. The Bible is listed first because it is our chief source of knowledge about God and Christ and contains all the truth necessary for salvation.

2. *God.* God is infinite in wisdom, power, and love—the creator and sustainer of the universe. Every person on earth is God's child. God will hear the prayer of any and every person. One does not have to go through any intermediary to reach God. However,

through worship in the sanctuary, through fellowship with other people, through proclamation of the faith from the pulpit, through study in classes, and in other ways, the church helps one learn about and commune with God.

3. *Jesus Christ.* "For God so loved the world that he gave his only Son" (John 3:16). We believe Jesus Christ is uniquely God's Son, sent by God, to be born of Mary, to make the invisible God known in human form. In his expressions of loving mercy, in his teaching, in his miracles of compassion, in the absolutely holy life he lived, in the compassion of his ministry, and in the utter selflessness of his servanthood, we see God. "Whoever has seen me has seen the Father," Jesus said (John 14:9).

We believe Jesus Christ died upon a cross for us and our sins. His cross is an example of sacrifice, and it is a revelation of God's love; but it is more, much more. His death on the cross forever makes a difference in a person's relationship with God. As Paul put it, "In Christ God was reconciling the world to himself" (2 Corinthians 5:19). We find salvation through his shed blood.

We believe Christ rose from the dead, and his resurrection is our assurance that there is life for us beyond the grave. "Because I live, you also will live" (John 14:19).

4. *The Holy Spirit.* The Holy Spirit is God here on this earth—God in us and with us. The Holy Spirit came in a new and mighty way upon the Christians at Pentecost (Acts 2) and is present in the world today. We believe the Spirit bears witness to our spirits that we are in Jesus Christ and are the children of God (Romans 8:16). "The witness of the Spirit" is a doctrine often emphasized by John Wesley. In his sermon on the subject, he said, "By the witness of the Spirit I mean the inward impression on the soul, whereby the Spirit of God immediately and directly witnesses to my spirit that I am a child of God; that Jesus Christ hath loved me and given Himself for me; that all my sins are blotted out and I, even I, am reconciled to God."

5. *Forgiveness of our sins and the salvation of our souls.* This is the very center of our faith. Sin is both in our nature and in our actions. It may be said that our actions are the expressions of the sin in our souls. If we are "heartily sorry for these our misdoings," as we pray in a prayer of confession, and put our faith in Jesus Christ, we are justified, saved, cleansed—not because we deserve it, but because of the grace, the unmerited favor of God. "Therefore, since we are justified by faith, we have peace with God through our Lord Jesus Christ" (Romans 5:1).

6. *Holiness.* As the result of commitment to God we grow in faith, and our love for God and for one another becomes more complete. Holiness of heart and life has always been emphasized by Methodists. Actually, no one ever attains a literal sinlessness in life. As one grows in Christian faith, the intentions of the soul become more perfect. This is what we call *sanctification.* "For those whom he foreknew he also predestined to be conformed to the image of his Son, in order that he might be the firstborn within a large family" (Romans 8:29).

7. *Conversion.* One becomes a Christian through the Christian experience of conversion. It may be a climactic experience such as came to Saul of Tarsus as he was on the way to Damascus. Suddenly he saw a light from heaven and heard the voice of Jesus (Acts 9, 22, 24). As long as he lived, that experience was the light of his life. Throughout the history of Methodism, there have been revivals when people "came forward" to the altar in a church or revival service and received a life-changing experience in Christ. Many Methodists have been able to sing:

> I can tell you now the time,
> I can take you to the place;
> Where the Lord saved men,
> By his wonderful grace.

But there is also the experience of Timothy. He never had a climactic conversion. He could not refer to any one moment when he was converted to Christ. Writing to Timothy, Paul said, "From childhood you have known the sacred writings that are able to instruct you for salvation through faith in Christ Jesus" (2 Timothy 3:15).

John Wesley as a child was carefully instructed in the Christian faith by his wonderful mother. Throughout his life, he never forgot his early teaching. Thus it is natural that from the very beginning of the Methodist societies he would give great emphasis to teaching children. Methodism has always practiced infant baptism. It is even argued by some that Wesley organized the very first Sunday schools, preceding Robert Raikes. Methodism strongly emphasizes teaching children. No church in the world today provides finer literature for children than does The United Methodist Church, which also provides careful instruction in membership for children. Children are happily received into full membership in the church.

In the early days of Methodism, new members came out of revivals. Today many persons professing their faith are youth who have grown up in the church and who are now making their profession of faith. Blessed is the church that remembers the words of our Lord, "Let the little children come to me, and do not stop them; for it is to such as these that the kingdom of heaven belongs" (Matthew 19:14).

Zacchaeus experienced yet a different type of conversion—a great decision. As Zacchaeus and Jesus visited together in his home, he decided to change his way of living. Jesus told him, "Today salvation has come to this house" (Luke 19:9).

Methodism has always been glad to accept the individual experience that each person has had.

8. *The Church.* The United Methodist Church recognizes and accepts all other Christian churches. We have embraced the openness that John Wesley affirmed when he preached on 2 Kings 10:15, "Is your heart as true to mine as mine is to yours? . . . If it is, give me your hand."

All Christians are invited to the Communion table in every United Methodist church. Methodism's invitation to participate in the sacrament of the Lord's Supper, or Holy Communion, is as follows:

Christ our Lord invites to his table all who love him, who earnestly repent of their sin and seek to live in peace with one another. Therefore, let us confess our sin before God and one another (*The United Methodist Hymnal,* page 7).

Methodism accepts both the baptism and vows of membership from any other Christian church. A person coming from another denomination is asked two questions: "As a member of Christ's universal church, will you be loyal to The United Methodist Church, and do all in your power to strengthen its ministries?" and "As a member of this congregation, will you faithfully participate in its ministries by your prayers, your presence, your gifts, and your service?"

Also, it has always been the custom of Methodist churches to cooperate with other churches in every possible way. Methodism has never claimed to be the only church. It claims to be *one* of the Christian churches. It has been pointed out by many that The United Methodist Church recognizes "the Christians of other churches and the churches of other Christians."

9. *Baptism.* Baptism is an outward sign of an inner commitment and a spiritual new birth. It is a rite of initiation into the body of which Christ is the head. It is believed that three modes of baptism were practiced by the early church: sprinkling, pouring, and immersion. We know that these three modes continue to be practiced by Christians today. Being more concerned about the inner experience than the outward expressions, The United Methodist Church both practices and accepts any mode of baptism. However, sprinkling is the method most often used in United Methodist churches.

FREEDOM FROM RIGID CREED

In reference to rigid creeds, Wesley made the following statement in a sermon in Glasgow:

There is no other religious society under Heaven which requires nothing of men in order to assure their admission into it but a desire to save their souls. Look all around you; you cannot be admitted into the Church, or Society of the Presbyterian, Anabaptists, Quakers, or any other unless you hold the same opinion with them, and adhere to the same mode of worship. The Methodists alone do not insist on your holding this or that opinion; but they think and let think. Neither do they impose any particular mode of worship; but you may continue to worship in your former manner, be it what it may. Now, I do not know any other religious society, either ancient or modern, wherein such liberty of conscience is now allowed, or has been allowed, since the age of the Apostles. Here is our glorying; and a glorying peculiar to us. What Society shares it with us?

The above quotation is rather long, but it is most important in understanding The United Methodist Church today. In Wesley's day, the church in England had had enough sectarian controversies. Methodism has from the beginning been more concerned with the warm heart and good life of the person. As one reads the twenty-five Articles of Religion of the church (see pages 23–34), one sees they are free from dogmatic definitions or requirements. The one thing required of those who desire admission into The United Methodist Church has always been a "desire to flee from the wrath to come and to be saved from their sins." However, that desire does imply certain convictions in the heart and mind of a person—especially belief in God, in Jesus Christ, and in the Bible as the sufficient rule of faith and practice. Methodism has always believed that few doctrines are essential—we "think and let think."

5

A SINGING CHURCH

We United Methodists speak often of John Wesley, but we sometimes forget Charles Wesley. After John Wesley's heart had been "strangely warmed," he first went to Charles; and it was to him he first said, "I believe." Later when they faced the question of whether or not the Methodist societies should sever their connection with the Church of England, it was Charles who said, "Church or no church, we must attend to the work of saving souls," though he was opposed to leaving the Church of England. It was Charles who so faithfully recorded the Christian experiences of those early Methodists as he wrote the hymns that they sang.

Through the years, Charles Wesley's hymns have been the binding cord of all Methodism. His hymns gave the Methodist movement life and warmth and heart. It was said of many a Methodist preacher: "He gathered a congregation about him by singing and, after prayer, began to preach."

We can never measure the influence of hymns on Methodism. It has been said over and over that where *one* reads the sermons of John, *a thousand* sing the hymns of Charles. The first hymn in *The United Methodist Hymnal* is Charles' "O for a Thousand Tongues to Sing"—indeed, that hymn is the keynote of Methodism.

> O for a thousand tongues to sing
> my great Redeemer's praise...
>
> My gracious Master and my God,
> assist me to proclaim...

There we have it—*praise* and *proclaim*. Those are the foundation stones of an evangelistic faith. Charles Wesley had wonderful poetic gifts that he used to do the work of an evangelist. He wrote and he sang:

A charge to keep I have,
a God to glorify,
a never-dying soul to save,
and fit it for the sky.

Today it is traditional to open a United Methodist annual conference with Charles' stirring hymn:

And are we yet alive,
and see each other's face?

One day Charles was standing at a window watching a storm. The rain was pouring down from the blackened skies. The wind was blowing hard. A dove fluttered up to the window, cold and frightened. Charles raised the window, took the little bird, and put it under his coat to get it dry and warm. Gently he stroked the bird; and when the storm had passed, he set it free. Out of that experience he wrote:

Jesus, lover of my soul,
let me to thy bosom fly,
while the nearer waters roll,
while the tempest still is high.
Hide me, O my Savior, hide,
till the storm of life is past;
safe into the haven guide;
O receive my soul at last.

With lusty enthusiasm he would sing his hymn "Soldiers of Christ, arise, / and put your armor on." With deep conviction he proclaimed, "I want a principle within / of watchful, godly fear." Joyfully he wrote and sang, "Love Divine, All Loves Excelling."

Charles Wesley wrote over six thousand hymns. He inspired Methodists to sing, and he still does.

As we proclaim the birth of our Lord, we sing Charles' hymn, "Hark! the Herald Angels Sing."

As we celebrate Jesus' death, we are glad Charles wrote:

O Love divine, what has thou done! . . .
bore all my sins upon the tree.
Th'immortal God for me hath died:
My Lord, my Love, is crucified.

On Easter morning we sing with joyous enthusiasm the hymn
Charles Wesley gave us—"Christ the Lord Is Risen Today."
Victoriously we sing the hymn he wrote:

Rejoice, the Lord is King!
Your Lord and King adore.

Many of us believe that had not Methodism been a singing
church, it would never have grown and expanded as it did. Singing
is a vital part of our church, and today we remember John Wesley's
Directions for Singing (*The United Methodist Hymnal*, page vii):

I. Learn these tunes before you learn any others; afterwards
learn as many as you please.

II. Sing them exactly as they are printed here, without alter-
ing or mending them at all; and if you have learned to sing
them otherwise, unlearn it as soon as you can.

III. Sing all. See that you join with the congregation as frequently as you can. Let not a slight degree of weakness or
weariness hinder you. If it is a cross to you, take it up, and
you will find it a blessing.

IV. Sing lustily and with a good courage. Beware of singing as
if you were half dead, or half asleep; but lift up your voice
with strength. Be no more afraid of your voice now, nor
more ashamed of its being heard, than when you sung the
songs of Satan.

V. Sing modestly. Do not bawl, so as to be heard above or dis-
tinct from the rest of the congregation, that you may not
destroy the harmony; but strive to unite your voices together, so as to make one clear melodious sound.

VI. Sing in time. Whatever time is sung be sure to keep with it.
Do not run before nor stay behind it; but attend close to
the leading voices, and move therewith as exactly as you
can; and take care not to sing too slow. This drawling way
naturally steals on all who are lazy; and it is high time to
drive it out from us, and sing all our tunes just as quick as
we did at first.

VII. Above all sing spiritually. Have an eye to God in every word you sing. Aim at pleasing him more than yourself, or any other creature. In order to do this attend strictly to the sense of what you sing, and see that your heart is not carried away with the sound, but offered to God continually; so shall your singing be such as the Lord will approve here, and reward you when he cometh in the clouds of heaven.

6

THE UNITED METHODIST CHURCH AND SOCIAL CONCERNS

When Methodism left the British Isles to cross the Atlantic, it left something it has been a long time in recovering—the deep social concerns of its founder. John Wesley believed both in the experience of faith and its practice—an emotional experience—a program of action. In his mind, the four greatest evils of his day were poverty, war, ignorance, and disease. For more than half a century he waged war on these enemies of society, and in his struggles the social conscience of today was born.

There are sufficient reasons why American Methodism did not carry the banner of Wesley's war against the enemies of society. Those social problems were not found in early America, which in the late 1700's was a rural frontier society. It was a land of boundless opportunity and for the most part a homogeneous society. The great need in America was evangelism, and those early Methodist circuit riders developed an evangelism unparalleled in the world, before or since. Revival fires were lighted, souls were saved, churches were established.

Now the situation in America has vastly changed. In our society there are poor and hungry people. In our population in the United States, there are people from every race and society of this earth; and prejudices need to be confronted. Today we face the threat of nuclear, biological, and chemical warfare with a power of destruction far greater than anything Wesley could ever imagine. Great progress has been made in the war against ignorance and disease, but there is still a long way to go.

Today, American Methodism is in the act of rediscovering our church's founder. If this chapter seems to be more labored than the others in this small volume, it is because the need just now in our society is so great. On social issues, let us be re-introduced to our church father.

WEALTH

What did Wesley say about *wealth?* We read again his sermon "The Use of Money," which sums up his view. We are to gain wealth only in ways that do not injure ourselves in mind or body, because to gain wealth in this way would be "buying gold too dear." Neither must our accumulation injure any other person.

However, wealth does not belong to the one who accumulates it. Only God owns; people are the stewards. We are to render unto God everything—"not a tenth, not a third, not half, but all that is God's." Caring for one's family is a part of God's work. Next, if "there be an overplus left," then "do good to them that are of the household of faith"; and "if there be an overplus still, 'do good unto all men.' "

Wesley had a severe doctrine of stewardship, and he felt that those who did not live by it "were not only robbing God, continually embezzling and wasting their Lord's goods, but also robbing the poor, the hungry, the naked; wronging the widow and the fatherless; and making themselves accountable for all the want, affliction, and distress which they may, but do not, remove." Strong words!

Wesley was so dedicated to his stewardship convictions that he could write: "If I leave behind me ten pounds...you and all mankind bear witness against me that I lived and died a thief and a robber." He practiced his philosophy and died practically in poverty. He believed that the poor had certain rights and that, when half the people were burdened by wealth and half by poverty, human rights had been robbed.

Wesley went far beyond the old "charity" attitude. More than any other person he was the founder of modern philanthropy. *Charity* relieves only the immediate pain. *Philanthropy* seeks to cure the diseases of society. Philanthropy recognizes one's debt to society. The broken pipes in society must be repaired so that the water of life can flow to all people.

The first stage in giving is *charity,* the second stage is *philanthropy;* but Wesley also referred to the third stage, *social justice,* which recognizes that all people have rights to the good things of God's earth without being made objects of either charity or philanthropy. Since the days of Wesley, the church has had a growing insight into the meaning of a Christian social order—one that gives both the weak and the less fortunate a proper opportunity.

In Wesley's day poverty was accepted either as God's will for the poor, a demonstration of the fact that there was not enough wealth for everybody, or evidence that the poor were lazy and did not want to work. In reference to poverty, Wesley said: "What remedy is there for this sore evil? Many thousand poor people are starving. Find them work, and you will find them meat. They will earn and eat their own bread. But how can the masters [employers] give them work without ruining themselves? Procure vent [sale] for what is wrought [made] and the masters [employers] give them as much work as they can do. And this would be done by sinking the price of provisions; for then people would have money to buy other things."

Some would condemn Wesley for seeming to advocate a controlled economy. It was not economic theories but human hurt that motivated him. He saw a woman "picking up from a dunghill stinking sprouts, and carrying them home for herself and her children." He saw another "gathering the bones which dogs had left in the streets." To him poverty was a national shame "in a land flowing, as it were, with milk and honey! abounding with all the necessities, the conveniences, the superfluities of life!" The nation must respond.

OUR SOCIAL CREED

We believe in God, Creator of the world; and in Jesus Christ, the Redeemer of creation. We believe in the Holy Spirit, through whom we acknowledge God's gifts, and we repent of our sin in misusing these gifts to idolatrous ends.

We affirm the natural world as God's handiwork and dedicate ourselves to its preservation, enhancement, and faithful use by humankind.

We joyfully receive for ourselves and others the blessings of community, sexuality, marriage, and the family.

We commit ourselves to the rights of men, women, children, youth, young adults, the aging, and people with disabilities; to improvement of the quality of life; and to the rights and dignity of racial, ethnic, and religious minorities.

We believe in the right and duty of persons to work for the glory of God and the good of themselves and others and in the protection of their welfare in so doing; in the rights to property as a trust from God, collective bargaining, and responsible consumption; and in the elimination of economic and social distress.

We dedicate ourselves to peace throughout the world, to the rule of justice and law among nations, and to individual freedom for all people of the world.

We believe in the present and final triumph of God's Word in human affairs and gladly accept our commission to manifest the life of the gospel in the world. Amen.

(*Book of Discipline*, 1996, pages 105–6)

EDUCATION

Wesley was a constant and determined enemy of ignorance. Long before his experience of the warm heart, he knew the meaning of the trained mind. The first ten years of his life were spent in the school his mother established in their home for her many children. She believed she could improve on the methods used in her day in instructing and governing children, and she proved it. Each child was expected to master the alphabet by the age of five.

Not only did Susanna Wesley teach her children the educational subjects, she also set apart an hour a week when she would meet with each child alone for prayer and religious instruction. Thus John Wesley grew up relating religion and education, and for him there was never any conflict between the two. In his heart and ministry, religion and education were married; and they always remained as one, each supporting the other.

For five years Wesley was a student in Charterhouse School, London. Then he attended Oxford University, where he received the degree of master of arts—equivalent to our Ph.D. today.

At Oxford he developed his daily plan of study, which was on Mondays and Tuesdays, Greek and Latin; on Wednesdays, logic and ethics; on Thursdays, Hebrew and Arabic; on Fridays, metaphysics and natural philosophy; on Saturdays, oratory and poetry; on Sundays, divinity.

He never stopped studying. During his ministry he published 440 books, tracts, and pamphlets. One of his most famous phrases he wrote while a student at Oxford: "Leisure and I have taken leave of each other"—and so it was all his life.

The undying contribution Wesley made to education was not in the realm of theory or techniques. The world has moved far beyond him in these areas. What gives Wesley an everlasting place in the history of education was his conviction that all are equal before God and therefore the poor are as much entitled to the blessings of an education as are the rich or the high-born. Green the historian said that Wesley "gave the first impulse to our popular education."

Wesley promoted planned studies for his preachers, literature for the masses of people, the Kingswood School for the sons of his preachers (today he would have included the daughters), and the development of the Sunday school. He established a school for the poor at the Foundry in London and one for orphans in Newcastle.

However, as Methodism moved to America, educational concerns were not nearly so strong. In fact, professional education for the ministry was suspect in American Methodism for a long time. Cokesbury College was established early; but when it was destroyed by fire in 1795, after eight years of not too successful operation, many Methodists thought it might be a sign that Methodists should not build colleges.

The first Methodist theological school was established in Newbury, Vermont, in 1841. It was moved to Concord, New Hampshire, in 1847 and was named Methodist General Bible Institute. In 1867, it was moved to Boston and in 1871 became the Boston University School of Theology. In 1854, Garrett Biblical Institute was founded in Evanston, Illinois, and Drew Theological Seminary in 1867 in New Jersey.

As the Methodist attitude toward education changed, the church began to found colleges—Randolph-Macon Woman's College, Lynchburg, Virginia, 1830; Wesleyan University, Middletown, Connecticut, 1831; Allegheny College, Meadville, Pennsylvania, 1817, which became associated with Methodist interests in 1833; Dickinson College, Carlisle, Pennsylvania, 1783, which became associated with Methodism in 1833. Expansion to the west and south was rapid; and by the time of the Civil War, Methodism had established thirty-four colleges that remain today.

The Evangelical Association founded Union Seminary in 1853 in New Berlin, Pennsylvania, which became Albright College and later Central Pennsylvania College in Reading. Plainfield College was founded in 1862 in Plainfield, Illinois, and in 1870 moved to Naperville, changing its name to North Central College in 1926. Other schools were founded in the Midwest and West, but only three of those founded before 1890 became permanent institutions.

The United Brethren founded Otterbein College in 1847 in Westerville, Ohio, and Lebanon Valley College, Annville,

Pennsylvania in 1866. Other schools were founded in the Midwest, some of which were merged or grew slowly.

In addition to colleges, there was a great need in America for high schools. Many Methodist academies were established and remained strong until public education met the need in their communities. Today The United Methodist Church has 104 colleges in 38 states and the District of Columbia. There are nine secondary schools and one elementary school. It has 13 seminaries, schools of theology, or graduate schools.

SUNDAY SCHOOLS

In speaking of education, let us not overlook the Sunday schools. The Sunday school offers both teaching and evangelistic opportunities. Many of us Methodists were carried to Sunday school as babies. We grew up feeling that we belonged. Before we ever learned to read, we were taught basic principles of the Christian faith; and many of us grew up believing ourselves to be Christians and never knowing ourselves to be anything else.

The educational process goes on throughout one's life. In The United Methodist Church, the Sunday school is concerned about every age, not only children. Methodism has a very effective program for youth. Another important emphasis today is on "singles," especially in metropolitan areas, where there are large numbers of single young adults. This group is an important part of any church program. Couples' classes, for both younger and older couples, are given much attention. There are intergenerational groupings. And in United Methodist Sunday schools, loving attention is given to older adult classes. The educational process covers the entire life span, and The United Methodist Church never gives up on the impossible task—the perfection of human character.

The *1996 Book of Discipline of The United Methodist Church* (page 469) provides for the General Board of Discipleship to "organize as may be necessary for carrying on the educational ministry throughout the whole life span of persons."

The board shall: have general oversight of the educational interests of the Church as directed by the General Conference. The board shall be responsible for the development of a clear statement of the biblical and theological foundations of Christian education, consistent with the doctrines of The United Methodist Church and the mission of the board. . . .

Through the ministry of Christian education, United Methodist congregations shall reach out to all persons as they are, encourage them to commit themselves to Christ and membership in his church, provide opportunities for them to grow in faith and to connect that faith with their daily lives, and equip them to live as God's people in the world.

All the concerns of the church are present in the Sunday school's educational ministry: Christian unity and interreligious concerns, church and society, evangelism, higher education, stewardship, worship, missions, and religion and race.

President Eisenhower once said, "I see no hope for the world except education, but I am most optimistic for the world because I believe in education." The United Methodist Church believes in education.

THE UNITED METHODIST PUBLISHING HOUSE

Supporting and undergirding the educational program of our churches is The United Methodist Publishing House.

According to legend, Martin Luther once threw his ink bottle at the devil. But John Wesley hurled an entire printing press at him! Francis Asbury wisely said that the religious press "is next in importance to the preaching of the gospel."

Four weeks after George Washington became President of the United States (March 4, 1789) twenty-five Methodist preachers met in John Street Chapel, New York City, and founded The Methodist Publishing House. However, the tradition of Methodist publishing goes back to John Wesley himself, who was constantly involved in the book business. He taught both preachers and lay people to read books and trained his preachers to sell books. He spent many hours editing classics for lay people, translating books from Latin, Greek, and German, so that Methodists could read the best that Christians had written through the ages. United Methodists should never forget that their founder was the most prolific author and publisher of his time. He earned and gave away $150,000 through publishing (equivalent to several million dollars today).

In America, John Dickins was the first book steward. The progress of this enterprise is indicated by the following quotation from *The Story of The Methodist Publishing House:* "At the time of unification [in 1939], the publishing interests of the Church consisted of two corporations of The Methodist Episcopal Church with houses in New York, Cincinnati, Chicago, Boston, Pittsburgh, Detroit, Kansas City, San Francisco, and Portland, Oregon; one corporation of the Methodist Episcopal Church, South with houses in Nashville, Dallas, and Richmond; and one corporation of the Methodist Protestant Church, with houses in Baltimore and Pittsburgh. The corporations were preserved under the new Board of Publication." Today there is one central headquarters of The United Methodist Publishing House, in Nashville, Tennessee, with 45 retail Cokesbury bookstores plus 30 academic bookstores at seminaries and universities.

The United Methodist Publishing House produces curriculum resources for The United Methodist Church and the ecumenical market. The production of books for scholars, pastors, and laity is an important ongoing ministry of the Publishing House. In addition, services for the church, such as bulletins, bulletin inserts, computer software, altar ware, robes, and a variety of other support products are offered by the House.

From the beginning, the proceeds of the Publishing House have provided pension help for retired United Methodist clergy and their dependents. Money is distributed to the annual conferences on a pro rata scale. Since the founding of the Publishing House, over $50,000,000 has been distributed to conference pension funds. This is a magnificent record of conscientious and successful management.

Each week vast numbers of pieces of literature are circulated in classes and groups within local church schools. This literature deals with lessons from the Bible, doctrines of the church, and problems that confront children, youth, adults, and the family. Able writers discuss social conditions and all manner of questions that arise in our complex civilization. No church surpasses ours in its literature, and few churches have reached our high standard of excellence and adaptability to the needs of these millions of people in country, village, and city. This great volume of wholesome reading matter is as good seed scattered abroad. Its influence in forming high ideals and molding Christian character cannot be overstated.

WESLEY AND WAR

Wesley was passionate in the denunciation of war. His conviction was that if people cannot settle their differences by reason and calm judgment, then certainly nothing would be settled by war. Wesley said:

Whatever be the cause, let us calmly and impartially consider the thing itself. Here are forty thousand men gathered together on this plain. What are they going to do? See, there are thirty or forty thousand more at a little distance. And these are going to shoot them through the head or body, to stab them or split their skulls, and send most of their souls into everlasting fire, as fast as they possibly can. Why so? What harm have they done to them? O none at all! They do not so much as know them. But, a man who is King of France, has a quarrel with another man, who is King of England. So these Frenchmen are to kill as many of these Englishmen as they can to prove the King of France is in the right. Now, what an argument is this! What a method of proof! What an amazing way of deciding controversies!

In Wesley's mind, war was totally against all reason and common sense. One can only wonder what he would say in reference to the destructive power of war today.

Methodism has always held high Wesley's banner—"The world is my parish." That means a loving concern for the welfare of each and every person on earth. War is the antithesis of universal love. Though Methodism has never embraced pacifism, though United Methodist churches proudly fly the flag of their country, though United Methodist people have gone forth in defense of their country—still Methodism stands firm in its support for peace on earth and good will toward all people.

Sherwood Eddy summed up the First World War in the words: "The saddest thing is not that some ten million of our people are dead, that the world is impoverished, victimized, embittered by hate, rent by suspicion and fear. The saddest thing is that we settled nothing, made nothing safe, achieved no lasting good."

One of the strongest satires against war is that which Mark Twain wrote in the form of a prayer:

O Lord our God, help us to tear their soldiers to bloody shreds with our shells;

Help us to cover their smiling fields with the pale forms of their patriot dead;

Help us to drown the thunder of the guns with the wounded, writhing in pain;

Help us to lay waste their humble homes with a hurricane of fire;

Help us to wring the hearts of their unoffending widows with unavailing grief;

Help us to turn them out rootless with their little children to wander unfriended through wastes of their desolate land;

For ourselves, who adore thee, Lord, blast their hopes, blight their lives, protract their bitter pilgrimage, make heavy their steps, water their way with their tears, stain the white snow with the blood of their wounded feet!

We ask of one who is the Spirit of Love and who is the ever faithful refuge and friend of those who are sorely beset, and seek his aid with humble and contrite hearts.

Grant our prayer, O Lord, and thine shall be the praise and honor and glory now and ever. Amen.

The reading of the above words strengthens us in our mission to join hands with people of good will over all the earth and to seek the elimination of all war.

Basil Mathews, walking in the dusty streets of an Arabian village, met a tall young Arab boy playing a flute. He asked to see the flute, for it seemed a heavy, awkward thing; on examining it, he found that it was made out of an old gun barrel. The boy explained that he had picked up an old gun on a nearby battlefield, filed it down, drilled holes in it, and out of a weapon of destruction had created an instrument of music.

"Swords into plowshares...spears into pruning hooks," wrote the prophet Micah (4:3). We can add, Weapons of destruction into instruments of music. Our church is dedicated to peace among all people.

HUMAN SUFFERING

As one reads even a few pages of Wesley's *Journal*, one can clearly see that the founder of Methodism was first concerned with the saving of souls; and his next consuming desire was to relieve people's physical distress and to see them well in body. Early in his ministry he had groups of volunteers carefully organized and regularly visiting the sick in London. He divided London into twenty-three sections and assigned two visitors to each section. Not only were they to bring comfort to the sick, these visitors were trained both to inquire into the spiritual state of the people and to discover their physical needs. The visitors were to seek medical advice and to try to provide for the physical needs of the people. Weekly the visitors were to report to the societies.

Wesley made arrangements for medicine for the poor and set aside Fridays for receiving the sick poor at his house in London. It was not long before "medicines were occasionally given to about five hundred persons." This service was not limited to members of the Society but was available for whoever needed it. Each Methodist society became an agency to serve the sick, the poor, and the needy.

Wesley's concern for the poor is seen in his writings. He published "A Collection of Recipes for the Use of the Poor." This was a compilation of simple remedies for the more common ailments. In 1747, he wrote and published "Primitive Physic: or an Easy and Natural Method of Curing Most Diseases."

It is no surprise that out of the church that Wesley established has come a great stream of serving institutions—hospitals, homes, and facilities for children, young people, those with disabilities, and the aging, all of which are under the Health and Welfare Ministries Department of the Board of Global Ministries. It is inspiring to realize that there are 72 hospitals in 26 states serving both the cause of medicine and The United Methodist Church.

Sixty-four United Methodist-related facilities in 31 states offer childcare to their communities. Many of these are homes for children with one or both parents missing. Some also offer help for unwed mothers. There are 256 retirement communities, homes, or nursing homes for the elderly run by Methodists in 40 states plus the District of Columbia

UNITED METHODISM AND RACIAL/ETHNIC ISSUES

United Methodists, and our predecessors, have long struggled with the difference between the challenge of the gospel and the reality of Christian life within culture. Nowhere has that been more obvious than in the struggle to be an inclusive church in a culture that values separation.

African slaves were brought to the colonies in 1620. From the beginning, Methodists struggled with the issue of slavery and the gospel. The Christmas Conference of 1784 included a ban on Methodists owning slaves, a ban that was never enforced because of objections from southern members. On the one hand, there were African American preachers in the church, such as Harry Hosier and Richard Allen. On the other hand, Richard Allen led a group of African American members to found what became the African Methodist Episcopal Church when they were asked to leave St. George's Church in Philadelphia.

In spite of the struggles, there were 145,000 African American members of the Methodist Episcopal Church in 1844, the year the church split over the issue of slavery. That number dropped to 30,000 in 1846, partly because many of the African American members were in the Methodist Episcopal Church, South. In 1870, the Colored Methodist Episcopal Church (now the Christian Methodist Episcopal Church) was organized for the African American members of the southern branch of Methodism.

When three branches of Methodism became The Methodist Church in 1939, the African American members were organized into a separate jurisdiction, the only one determined by race rather than geography. In 1968, this Central Jurisdiction was abolished; and those churches became part of geographic jurisdictions. The struggle for inclusivity still continues today, as we try to deal with the reality of racism within the church itself.

Methodist work with Native Americans began with John Wesley, during his short stay in Georgia. Methodist preachers were involved in outreach and education programs with Native Americans throughout the nineteenth century. For example, John Stewart and James B. Finley had a successful ministry with the Wyandots in Ohio. Thomas, William, and Sarah Johnson and Jerome Berryman went from Missouri to work with the eastern nations that had been removed to Kansas. Missionaries went to Oregon in response to an invitation from the nations in that area. Others worked with Native American communities in the Southwest. Methodist preachers moved with the southeastern nations to Oklahoma along the Trail of Tears.

On the other hand, Methodists were equally active in working for the removal of Native Americans in order to claim their land. Like the rest of our nation, United Methodists have much in our history with Native Americans for which to repent. We also have a strong Native American constituency focused in the Oklahoma Indian Conference and in places like McCurdy School in New Mexico.

Historic work with Hispanic Americans in the Southwest includes institutions such as Lydia Patterson Institute and the growing Rio Grande Conference. United Methodists work with immigrants from Mexico, Cuba, Puerto Rico, many countries in Central America, and the Caribbean. Sadly, United Methodists are also among those who want to deny political and social benefits even to legal immigrants and are among those who exploit immigrant laborers.

Methodists have worked with immigrants from Asia as well, establishing churches, schools, clinics, and other services. Methodists also have been involved in exploiting Chinese labor, the interning of Japanese Americans in camps during World War II, and attempting to treat Asian Americans as second-class citizens. Today, there are strong United Methodist churches among Korean, Japanese, Chinese, Vietnamese, and Filipino Americans.

❦

Wesley's life, his preaching, and his entire ministry became a proclamation of social Christianity. He said: "Solitary religion is not to be found [in the Gospel of Christ]. 'Holy Solitaire is a phrase no more consistent with the Gospel than holy adulterers. The Gospel of Christ knows no religion but social; no holiness but social holiness. . . . This we have from Christ that he who loves God, loves his brother also. . . . He feels in his soul a burning restless desire of spending and being spent for them."

Let it be emphasized that today United Methodism has a social mission. The term *social gospel* unfortunately implies to some people that there are two gospels—one social and the other individual. Let us reaffirm the fact that there is only one gospel. Christianity is a social religion in the sense that when an individual experiences Christ, that individual has a changed attitude toward society. Until the world and society in which we live can be called the kingdom of God, then Methodism will have a social mission.

JURISDICTIONAL BOUNDARIES
Within the United States

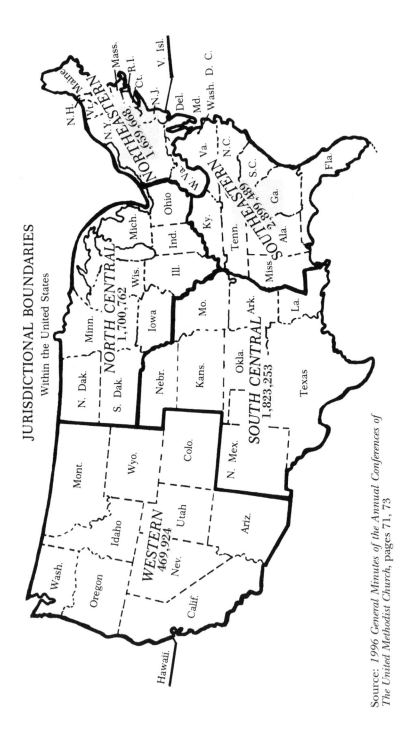

NORTHEASTERN
1,659,668

NORTH CENTRAL
1,700,762

SOUTHEASTERN
2,889,486

SOUTH CENTRAL
1,823,253

WESTERN
469,924

N.H.

Maine

Vt.

Mass.

R.I.

Ct.

N.Y.

N.J.

Del.

Md.

Wash. D. C.

V. Isl.

Va.

W. Va.

N.C.

S.C.

Ga.

Fla.

Ala.

Tenn.

Ky.

Miss.

Ohio

Ind.

Mich.

Ill.

Wis.

Iowa

Mo.

Ark.

La.

Minn.

N. Dak.

S. Dak.

Nebr.

Kans.

Okla.

Texas

N. Mex.

Colo.

Mont.

Wyo.

Idaho

Utah

Nev.

Ariz.

Calif.

Oregon

Wash.

Hawaii

Source: *1996 General Minutes of the Annual Conferences of
The United Methodist Church, pages 71, 73*

7

THE UNITED METHODIST CHURCH GOVERNMENT

From the beginning, The United Methodist Church and its fore-runners have been well organized. At the organization in 1784, all powers resided in that body of preachers. They had the authority to enact or repeal any legislation. At first it was planned to have a conference of all the preachers once a year. Bishop Francis Asbury adopted the custom of holding the yearly conference by sections across the church. That plan did not turn out to be practical, so an effort was made to govern the church through a council of presiding elders. Then, in 1792, a General Conference was called; and the quadrennial General Conference was created. It was to be a conference including all the preachers. However, due to the rapid growth of the church and the distances to be traveled, the General Conference of 1808 created our present plan of government by a delegated General Conference. This meant that annual conferences remote from the site of the General Conference would be equally represented. The first delegated conference was in 1812.

In 1870, the College of Bishops was assigned judicial as well as executive functions. This gave to the College of Bishops powers not unlike those of the US Supreme Court. In 1934, the General Conference officially set up the Judicial Council, which became a part of The Methodist Church. The Judicial Council is composed of five ministers and four lay persons, and "all appellate power" is vested in this council. All decisions of the Judicial Council are final. This is Methodism's Supreme Court.

In The United Methodist Church there are now six types of conferences. Certain duties or functions are assigned to each conference by the General Conference. The conferences are as follows:

1. The General Conference, which meets once in four years;
2. The Jurisdictional Conference, which meets once in four years;

61

3. The Annual Conference, which meets once a year;
4. The District Conference;
5. The Charge Conference;
6. The Church Conference.

THE GENERAL CONFERENCE

The General Conference is the one lawmaking body of The United Methodist Church. It alone can speak for the church. It determines the conditions, privileges, and duties of church membership; the powers and duties of the other conferences of the church; and the nature, function, and qualification of the ordained ministry. The General Conference is authorized to initiate and direct all connectional enterprises of the church and to provide boards for their promotion and administration.

The General Conference meets every four years and is composed equally of lay and ministerial members (about nine hundred), who have been elected by the annual conferences. The General Conference is subject to the Restrictive Rules, which are part of the Constitution of the church. They provide that

1. The General Conference shall not revoke, alter, or change our Articles of Religion. . . .
2. The General Conference shall not revoke, alter, or change our Confession of Faith.
3. The General Conference shall not change or alter any part or rule of our government so as to do away with episcopacy or destroy the plan of our itinerant general superintendency.
4. The General Conference shall not do away with the privileges of our clergy of right to trial by a committee and of an appeal; neither shall it do away with the privileges of our members of right to trial before the church, or by a committee, and of an appeal.
4. The General Conference shall not revoke or change the General Rules. . . .
5. The General Conference shall not appropriate the net income of the publishing houses, the book concerns, or the Chartered Fund to any purpose other than for the benefit of retired or disabled preachers, their spouses, widows, or widowers, and children. . . .

(*Book of Discipline*, pages 26-27)

THE JURISDICTIONAL CONFERENCE

The United Methodist Church has five jurisdictional conferences: Northeastern, Southeastern, North Central, South Central, and Western. The annual conferences in each jurisdiction elect the delegates to the jurisdictional conference; delegates are comprised equally of ministers and lay persons. The primary functions of each jurisdictional conference are to elect bishops, to determine boundaries of episcopal areas, to assign bishops, and to implement General Conference legislation.

THE ANNUAL CONFERENCE

As the name indicates, the annual conference of each designated area meets once a year. Not only is this conference composed of ministerial members, but every church or charge is represented by delegates who are laypersons. This is the basic body in the church. It votes on all constitutional amendments; elects delegates to General and jurisdictional conferences; has responsibility for all matters relating to ministerial character and orders; hears reports of councils, committees, boards, and agencies; and lays plans for the work of the coming year. The bishop in charge presides over the annual conference. The pastoral appointments are made at this conference, though pastors may be assigned at other times.

THE DISTRICT CONFERENCE

A district conference shall be held if directed by the annual conference of which it is a part and may be held upon the call of the district superintendent. A district conference shall be composed of members determined and specified by the annual conference. This conference may administer district real and personal property, form a district lay program, and "organize to develop, administer, and evaluate the missional life, advocacy needs, and ministries of the Church in and through the district" (*Book of Discipline*, page 387). There are a district committee on ordained ministry, a committee on district superintendency, and district organizations named United Methodist Women and United Methodist Men.

THE CHARGE CONFERENCE

The charge conference is made up of members of the church council (or councils, if more than one church is on the pastoral charge). The district superintendent, or a minister whom he or she designates, presides at the meetings. This conference meets annually and at other times when it is called. It has general supervision of the work of the local church.

THE CHURCH CONFERENCE

This conference is open to all members of the church and may consider any matter pertaining to the local church. Regulations governing the call and conduct of the charge conference also apply to the church conference.

CENTRAL CONFERENCES

Central conferences are those conferences of The United Methodist Church outside the United States. They have their own bishops and administrative officers, determine the boundaries of the annual conferences within their respective areas, and implement the legislation of the General Conference.

GENERAL COUNCIL ON MINISTRIES

The General Council on Ministries has as its purpose the facilitation of the church's program life, as outlined by the General Conference. It encourages, coordinates, and supports the general agencies in their work for the denomination. Membership on the council includes representation from all the jurisdictions in the United States, plus five persons from the central conferences, six bishops, two youth, one young adult, and ten members at large. The Council works with the General Boards of Church and Society, Discipleship, Global Ministries, and Higher Education and Ministry, plus the General Commissions on Archives and History, Communication, Christian Unity and Interreligious Concerns, Religion and Race, Status and Role of Women, Central Conference Affairs, and United Methodist Men.

GENERAL COUNCIL ON FINANCE AND ADMINISTRATION

The General Council on Finance and Administration is amenable to the General Conference. It receives and disburses all general church funds and works with all the general agencies in matters pertaining to budgets and fiscal responsibilities.

COUNCIL OF BISHOPS

The United Methodist Church is "episcopal" in its form of government. The bishops are the chief executives and administrative leaders of the church. They serve for life and assume "residential and presidential" duties until their retirement on or before their seventieth birthday. In addition to presiding over local conferences, they give churchwide and ecumenical leadership. Throughout the history of the church our bishops have both deserved and received honor and respect, and we look to our bishops for leadership.

THE DISTRICT SUPERINTENDENT

The district superintendent is appointed by the bishop from among the ministers of the annual conference to supervise the work of a given district. Districts may vary in size from about twenty pastoral charges in sparsely settled areas to sixty or more in metropolitan areas. The district superintendent is appointed each year but may be reassigned for a maximum of six successive years. The district superintendent travels and preaches throughout the district, supervises the affairs of the churches in the district, represents the pastors and churches of the district in the bishop's cabinet, and helps plan and support the work of the entire conference.

MINISTRIES OF DEACONS AND ELDERS

In The United Methodist Church, there are specialized ministries of deacon and elder. Deacons are ordained clergy who lead the church in relating faith and worship to life and ministry in the world. Deacons teach and preach the Word; lead in worship, assist elders in the administration of the sacraments, conduct weddings and funerals, and help lead the congregation in mission and witness in the world. The order of deacon is the result of a long development through the offices of deaconess, home missionary, and diaconal minister. Deacons are appointed to their place of service by the bishop, but deacons themselves may initiate the contacts that lead to an appointment. That is, they may work out their own assignment with local churches or agencies. If the assignment is approved, the bishop then makes the appointment.

Elders are committed to serve as itinerating clergy, that is, to be sent where the needs of the church and their gifts for ministry are judged by the bishop and the cabinet to be a good "fit." Most elders serve as pastors of local churches; but they also serve as chaplains, in general and conference agencies, and in administrative roles in the annual conference. As pastors, they are responsible for the total ministry of the local church in its nurturing ministries and in fulfilling its mission of witness and service in the world. To this end, they train and equip the laity to be in mission. They are responsible that the faith of the church is both preached and taught faithfully. They administer the business affairs of the congregation. Elders are guaranteed an appointment and agree to serve where the bishop determines they are most needed.

COMMITTEE ON PASTOR-PARISH RELATIONS

The committee on pastor-parish relations, composed of not fewer than five and not more than nine laypersons, is elected by the charge conference. This committee counsels with the pastor and other staff members; makes recommendations to the church council as to persons to be employed; consults on matters pertaining to pulpit supply, and proposals for salaries and other compensations; and cooperates with the pastor(s), the district superintendent, and the bishop in securing clergy leadership. Its relationship to the district superintendent and the bishop is advisory only.

TRUSTEES AND CHURCH PROPERTY

Each local church or charge must have a board of trustees, which holds the property of the church in trust and acts according to the will of the charge or church conference. The trust clause in deeds to church and parsonage property provides that the property is under the direction of The United Methodist Church.

THE CHURCH COUNCIL

The church council is responsible for planning and carrying out a program of nurture, outreach, and witness in the local church and for administering the business affairs of the church. It is accountable to the charge conference and carries out the goals and mission established by the charge conference.

UNITED METHODIST WOMEN

The organization of United Methodist Women is a part of the local church, and membership is open to any woman who indicates her desire to belong and to participate in the global mission of the church. Throughout many, many years, the organized women in the church have made important contributions.

Many churches also have an organization of United Methodist Men.

8

UNITED METHODISM'S WORLD MISSION

The development of the missionary zeal in Methodism may be summarized in three of Wesley's own statements: "About a quarter before nine...I felt my heart strangely warmed"; "I am a Priest of the Church Universal"; and "The world is my parish."

Our United Methodist Church in America came into being because of the missionary spirit, and our church has never lost its mission vision. No obstacle has been able to halt the Methodist missionaries. "Go therefore and make disciples of all nations, baptizing them in the name of the Father and of the Son and of the Holy Spirit, and teaching them to obey everything that I have commanded you. And remember, I am with you always, to the end of the age" (Matthew 28:19-20). This is a command of Jesus Christ that The United Methodist Church takes literally.

The Board of Global Ministries of The United Methodist Church is working either directly, or through ecumenical cooperation or partnership,* in the following countries:

Africa

Algeria	Burundi
Angola	Cameroon
Benin	Cape Verde Islands
Botswana	Chad
Burkina Faso	Comoro Islands

* *Ecumenical cooperation* means working with other denominational partners in an area or project; *partnership* means working with a Christian church in the country. For example, a United Methodist pastor from Oklahoma spent a year in Russia working with the Russian Orthodox Church on youth ministry and campus ministry.

Egypt	Namibia
Eritrea	Niger
Ethiopia	Nigeria
Gabon	Rwanda
Ghana	Senegal
Guinea-Bissau	Sierra Leone
Ivory Coast	Somalia
Kenya	South Africa
Liberia	Sudan
Madagascar	Swaziland
Malawi	Tanzania
Mauritania	Togo
Mauritius	Tunisia
Mozambique	Uganda

Asia

Afghanistan	Nepal
Bangladesh	Pakistan
Cambodia	Philippines
Hong Kong	Republic of China
India	Singapore
Indonesia	South Korea
Japan	Sri Lanka
Laos	Taiwan
Malaysia	Thailand
Myanmar	Vietnam

Middle East

Cyprus	Lebanon
Iraq	Turkey
Israel	West Bank and Gaza Strip
Jordan	

Europe

Austria
Belgium
Bosnia
Bulgaria
Commonwealth
  of Independent
  States
Croatia
Czech and Slovak
  Republics
Denmark
Estonia
Eurasia
Finland
France
Germany
Greece
Herzegovina

Hungary
Ireland
Italy
Latvia
Lithuania
Macedonia
Norway
Poland
Portugal
Republic of Georgia
Romania
Russia
Spain
Sweden
Switzerland
Ukraine
(former) Yugoslavia

The Caribbean

Abaca
Antigua
Aruba
Bahamas
Barbados
Belize
Bonaire
Cuba
Curacao
Dominica
Dominican
  Republic

Guadeloupe
Haiti
Jamaica
Martinique
Puerto Rico
St. Lucia
St. Vincent and the
  Grenadines
Tobago
Trinidad
Virgin Islands

Pacific

Polynesia	Melanesia
Guam	Micronesia
Samoa	
Tahiti	
Tonga	

The Americas

Argentina	Guyana
Brazil	Honduras
Bolivia	Mexico
Chile	Nicaragua
Colombia	Panama
Costa Rico	Peru
Ecuador	United States
El Salvador	Uruguay
Guatemala	Venezuela

A PERSONAL EXPRESSION

I love The United Methodist Church because

The church sent her itinerant ministers into the mountain areas of the Southeast and won my ancestors to a life of piety and service as disciples of Jesus Christ.

The church sought my father in those distant hills, put something into his heart, claimed his life, and gave him a place of service as a Methodist preacher. The night he died, he said to me, "It's all right. I have the faith."

The church brought a young girl into the fellowship, gave to her the highest ideals, a beautiful and dedicated Christian spirit. She was my mother.

The church quickly claimed me for the kingdom of God and gave me opportunities to go to school and to fulfill my mission in life as a preacher.

The church brought me into fellowship with Christian people and into fellowship with God. The church led me to believe in Jesus Christ and to accept him as my Savior and Lord.

The church blessed my marriage and helped my wife and me to claim our children for Christ.

The United Methodist Church is the best thing that ever happened to me.

I love my church.

Charles L. Allen

Meet the Methodists

STUDY GUIDE

John O. Gooch

1

THE CHURCH

1. Begin with a community-building exercise. Ask each group member to introduce herself or himself by answering three questions: Who am I? How am I? What do I bring to this session? For example, one person might say, "My name is Linda Davis. I'm totally exhausted because of pressures at my work. I bring enough curiosity and interest to get me here even though I'd rather be at home."

2. Next, ask: What if the church did not exist? (Not just our congregation, but the Christian church as a whole. No churches anywhere.)
How would the world be different?
What would be missing?

Then ask: If the church did not exist, what difference would that make to you?
What is important about the church in your life?

OR

What could the church do that would make a difference for your life?

List the group members' answers to the above questions on a chalkboard or large piece of paper. Invite the group members to look at the list "Why the Church?" on pages 13–15.

Ask: Which of these reasons would you want to add to your list? Why?

3. Have a scavenger hunt. Form teams of no more than three per-

sons each. Tell the teams that they have ten minutes (or fifteen, depending on the size of your building) to go through the church building and to make a list of all the ministries of the church they can find. Some of these ministries will be happening in other parts of the building, some will be announced in the bulletin, some will have displays on bulletin boards, some will have signs on the doors of rooms. The team should be able to identify where in the building they saw evidence of each ministry on the list. Announce that there will be a "prize" for the team with the longest list of ministries. (Have a prize that can be shared with all present.)

OR

If your group members would be reluctant to have a scavenger hunt, take them on a tour of the building, pointing out indications of the ministries of the church.

Whichever option you choose, debrief by asking: Do these ministries make the church worthwhile? Why or why not?

4. Ask: Is it true that there is "no such thing as a solitary religion"? Can we be just as religious without the church?
Can we be just as Christian without the church?
What is the difference between being "religious" and being a Christian?

5. Say: The Apostles' Creed states that we believe in the "holy catholic church, the communion of saints." What does that mean to you?

[Note to Leader: *Catholic* means "universal" and not the church of Rome. For the church to be *holy* means that we try to reflect the nature of our God, who is holy. This does not mean, however, that we have to live up to some impossible moral perfection or spiritual overachievement. Rather it means that we try to be open to God in order that we can become more like God.]

Say: The creed says that the "holy catholic church" is also the "communion of saints." Saints, in the New Testament, are people who are members of the church, people who are "on the way." Therefore Paul can refer to the church in Rome as "God's beloved in Rome, who are called to be saints" (Romans 1:7).

Invite persons to share memories of times when the community of the church was important to them. Their answers might include support in a time of crisis or great joy or the awareness of the church working together to serve persons in need.

6. Close with a brief prayer of thanks for the group and for discoveries made about the church.

2

THE UNITED METHODIST CHURCH

Before the session, gather copies of newspapers and news magazines (as current as possible), so that each person in the group can have one. Also gather scissors and tape. On a chalkboard or four large pieces of paper, make four columns, headed "Poverty," "War," "Ignorance," and "Disease."

1. Repeat the community-building exercise from Session 1. Ask persons to introduce themselves by answering three questions: Who am I? How am I? What do I bring to this session?

2. Tell the group that United Methodists (and our predecessor bodies) have always been committed to a "warm heart," clear thinking about what we believe, and an active religion. We will look at all of these emphases in this session but will focus on what United Methodists believe in Session 4.

3. Remind the group members that Wesley never intended to start a new church. He wanted his followers to remain in the Church of England as "societies" within that body. Review the account of the rise of the societies found on pages 21–22.

Then say: There was only one requirement if you wanted to become a member of the Society. What was it? (A desire for salvation.) Tell the group that this is the "warm heart" part of our tradition.

4. Ask: What were the requirements if you wanted to continue in the Society? (These three requirements form the outline of "The General Rules," which are still valid for United Methodists today.)

5. Ask: Do you think it is important to have requirements for membership?

Why or why not?

To what other organizations, service clubs, and so on, do you belong?

What requirements for membership do they have?

What do you think requirements for remaining in the church should be? (Allow a sufficient length of time for the group members to consider this question. There may be some reluctance to respond at first since this is a type of question most of us do not think about often. Be comfortable with silence and trust your question.)

After the group has had time to discuss that question, say: Actually, United Methodists have some requirements both for joining the church and for continuing in it. When we become members of The United Methodist Church, we promise that we will: pray for the church, be in attendance at worship, be faithful stewards of our money and other possessions, and be involved in ministry and mission. Some people argue that the vows also assume participation in some form of Christian education.

Ask: Do these membership requirements seem unreasonable ?

What if we enforced them strictly?

Could we remove persons from the rolls if they did not make a pledge to the budget, for example? if they did not actively participate in some kind of ministry/mission?

Would that be a good thing? (Note that some service clubs routinely remove members who do not attend.)

6. Note the lists of what United Methodists believe (pages 19 and 23–24).

Ask: Are there statements here about which you have questions or concerns?

How can we plan to look for answers before Session 4, when we will focus on beliefs?

7. Distribute copies of newspapers and news magazines, together with scissors and tape. Ask persons to find stories dealing with poverty, war, ignorance, and disease. Have them cut out the stories and tape them to the chalkboard or large pieces of paper. When all have

finished, say that Wesley considered these to be the greatest evils of his day and did everything in his power to overcome them. The church today continues to work to eliminate poverty, war, ignorance, and disease.

Tell the group that this is the proof of religion.

Ask: Does it result in ministry to those who cannot stand on their own?

Does it result in concerted action to overcome evils, such as war and disease, that threaten humanity?

8. Close with prayer.

3

METHODISM IN AMERICA

Before the session, find a large map of the United States, purchase some pushpins (preferably in different colors), or cut small pennants out of colored paper to tape onto the map. *National Geographic* maps, or large road maps, would be good sources for the map. If you can find a "family tree" of United Methodism, showing the divisions and reunions in the denomination, display it as well.

If you plan to show the video, *Our United Methodist Heritage,* be sure you have it ordered and that a VCR and a monitor are available.

On the chalkboard or a large piece of paper, list the following events and dates:

American Revolution, 1775–83
Election of George Washington, 1789
Louisiana Purchase, 1803
Mexican War, 1846–47
Gold discovered in California, 1849
Large-scale emigration to the Oregon country, 1840's
War Between the States, 1861–65

1. Begin by saying that this session tracks the incredible spread of United Methodism and its predecessors across the United States. Ask for one or two volunteers to mark places on the map. Other persons in the group should plan to help identify "states and dates" as we move through history. Point out also how the spread of Methodism has paralleled the history and westward expansion of the United States, using the chart you have prepared.

Mark the colonies (Maryland, New York, Pennsylvania) whose

churches sent delegates to the first annual conference in 1773. Ask for names of persons associated with those churches. If you know, or someone in your congregation knows, more details about these persons, invite them to tell stories about them.

Francis Asbury arrived in America in 1771. Take time to tell something about Asbury—at least that he was one of only two Methodist preachers who stayed in America during the Revolution, that he was the first bishop in American Methodism, and that he built American Methodism on a system of itinerant preaching. Add pushpins for Boston and Virginia to the map.

Remind the group that between 1771 and 1784 there was a great war in the colonies. Ask someone to describe the growth in American Methodism in those years.

Put in pushpins on the map for the Carolinas, Georgia, Tennessee, Kentucky, and Ohio by 1789, when George Washington became our first President.

In 1803, the United States more than tripled in size, with the purchase of Louisiana. In 1804, there were Methodist preachers in Indiana, Illinois, Michigan, and Missouri. Ask for a report on the growth of Methodism by the time Asbury died in 1816. Add pushpins for the other states east of the Mississippi not already covered.

Texas became part of the United States in 1845, and gold was discovered in California in 1849. This opened the Southwest to Methodist missionaries. In the 1830's and 1840's, Methodist churches were started in Iowa, Nebraska, and Kansas (including a strong mission to Native Americans in Kansas).
Add pushpins for all those states. Add Oregon and California in 1848, Colorado in 1859, the Dakotas, Idaho, Montana, Nevada, Utah, Wyoming, and Arizona by 1865.

Ask for comments, reflections, or questions on the growth of Methodism in those years.

2. Call attention to the founding and growth of The United Brethren Church (pages 31–32). Be sure the group is aware of the names of Philip Otterbein and Martin Boehm and the famous *"Wir*

sind Bruder" meeting. Note the growth in the United Brethren from 1815 to 1920.

3. Note also the founding and growth of the Evangelical Association, beginning with Jacob Albright.

4. If you have a copy of the United Methodist "family tree," point out how our ancestors divided and came back together. Where you can, give some reasons for the divisions and the reunions.

OR

1–4. If you can secure a copy of the video *Our United Methodist Heritage* (35 minutes), plan to show it. This video traces our heritage from the Reformation through American Methodism. It is available on a rental basis from EcuFilm (800-251-4091) or may be available through your conference resource center.

5. If possible, introduce information about the history of your local church at the proper point in the session. Did your church begin as a member of one of the predecessor bodies, or has it always been a United Methodist Church? Has it always been in its current location? Who were some of its early leaders, lay and clergy?

If you do not know your church's history, you may want to assign a group member to seek information and report at the next session.

6. Close with a prayer of thanksgiving for our heritage and a petition that we might continue to be faithful to God's calling.

4

WHAT UNITED
METHODISTS BELIEVE

For this session, you will need a chalkboard, or several large pieces of paper, in addition to a copy of *Meet the Methodists* for each member of the group.

1. Tell the group that the openness of United Methodism has often led people to say things such as, "You don't have to believe anything to be a Methodist." Ask the group to turn to "Freedom From Rigid Creed" on pages 41–42 and to read the quotation from Wesley's sermon found there.

Ask: What did Wesley say was the "glory" of the Methodists? Why did he say that?

Say: Notice that Wesley did not say that Methodists do not have to believe anything. He said that we do not insist on beliefs so rigid that they divide us. The key is our relationship to Christ and how we live out that relationship in the world.

2. Tell the group that, when Wesley was asked what the Methodists believed, he said, "We believe in the creeds." By that he meant the Apostles' Creed and the Nicene Creed.

Invite the group to turn to page 35 in *Meet the Methodists*. Point out the "seven beliefs" found in the Apostles' Creed. Form seven small teams, one for each of the seven beliefs. (Note: If you have a small group, each person can be a team, or you can assign two of the beliefs on the list to a single team.) Ask each team to look at the four creeds printed in the book and to summarize what each says about the assigned belief (or beliefs).

While participants are working, make a chart on the chalkboard or on several large pieces of paper. Make seven columns, each headed by one of the beliefs on page 35. Make four rows, one for each of the four creeds. (Leave plenty of space in the rows for writing.)

After ten to fifteen minutes for the teams to work, ask for reports. List findings on the chart.

Ask: What do all the creeds have in common?
Are there differences?
If so, what are they?
What do you think the differences mean?

Say: Because the Nicene and Apostles' creeds are ancient affirmations of the church, nearly all Christians agree on their importance as statements of faith. The differences in beliefs stem from other issues or from different emphases on issues. We will look at some distinctive United Methodist beliefs next.

3. Invite the group to look at the United Methodist beliefs summarized on pages 37–41. Ask them to stay in the same seven teams, and ask each team to report on one of the topics listed. Encourage them not only to summarize what is said but also to raise questions they have about the topic and/or to list points where they know Christians (and/or denominations) disagree on an issue. For example, all Christians would say that the Bible is the inspired Word of God, but not all Christians agree on what *inspiration* means.

Ask: Where have persons in the group been aware of differences in understanding that caused serious problems between Christians?

Again, allow ten to fifteen minutes for this work; then ask for reports. List questions and concerns on the chalkboard or a large piece of paper. Spend some time talking about the questions and any other issues about belief members of the group want to raise. If there are more questions than you can handle in the time available, or if you are not sure about some of the answers, plan with the group how you will deal with the questions. Your pastor or church library are possible sources of information.

4. Close with a prayer of thanksgiving for people who worked faithfully in the past to help us understand our faith and for persons today who are willing to struggle with faith questions.

5

A SINGING CHURCH

Ahead of time, gather copies of *The United Methodist Hymnal.* If your church has a music director, invite him or her to be a part of this session.

1. Tell the group that Charles Wesley wrote many of his hymns to popular tunes of his day. (The laws about copyrights and plagiarism did not exist in the eighteenth century!) Suggest that you try to do the same thing.

Form teams of two or three persons. Have each team pick a faith topic from Chapter 4, "What United Methodists Believe." Then have them select a popular song whose tune is familiar to all the members of the team. Finally, ask them to write one verse of a hymn about the topic, to be sung to that tune. (Reassure the teams that this is not something they have to do to performance level. It is only an activity to help them experience how illiterate miners were able to sing Charles Wesley's hymns so easily.)

2. When the teams have finished, tell them that the way hymns were sung in Wesley's day was far different from the way we sing. They sang outdoors, with no accompaniment, no speaker systems, and no printed words. This was also true on the American frontier. What they did was "line the hymns." The leader sang one or two lines, and the congregation sang them back. Then the leader sang one or two more, and so on. Remember the tunes were familiar, they only had to grasp the words.

Ask if any team would like to demonstrate by lining its hymn for the group to sing. (Allow as many teams as will volunteer to lead.)

Ask: Can you see how easy it would be to teach the faith by singing it? What do you carry in your heads more easily—what the preacher said last Sunday or a song that's fun to sing? Tell the group that John Wesley said, so long as the Methodists sang Charles' hymns and those of Isaac Watts, it did not matter what the preacher said—the Methodists would have a sound theology.

3. Distribute copies of *The United Methodist Hymnal*. Ask persons to turn to the Table of Contents (page viii) and to notice how the categories of hymns match the basic doctrines of United Methodism that we saw in Chapter 4.

Ask: What categories are listed here that we did not find in Chapter 4?

What topics do you see in the Table of Contents that pique your curiosity?

Invite persons to browse through the hymnal, looking for (1) familiar hymns, (2) personal favorites, and (3) hymns on topics of interest.

4. If your congregation has a music director, ask her or him to meet with the group to talk about topics such as how hymns are chosen for worship, the part that music plays in the church, hymns and anthems as ways to teach the faith, and other topics he or she might want to present.

5. Since you are already into singing, close by singing one of the great hymns of the Wesleyan heritage, such as "O For a Thousand Tongues to Sing," "Love Divine, All Loves Excelling," or "A Charge to Keep I Have."

6

THE UNITED METHODIST CHURCH AND SOCIAL CONCERNS

1. Remind the group that Wesley considered that the great evils of his day were poverty, war, ignorance, and disease. He also believed that, when one became a Christian, one needed to make changes in one's way of life, including the structures of society. In today's session, we will look at those evils and how The United Methodist Church deals with them. Faith should make a difference in life.

2. Look first at the issue of poverty. In the late 1990's, the nation's welfare system was being drastically cut back; and the churches were faced with the issue of hands-on, personal responsibility for the needs of the poor.

Ask: What ministries for working with the poor do we have in our congregation? (For example, Room in the Inn, a food bank, Habitat for Humanity, community services.)
Do those ministries meet the definition of the understanding of charity, philanthropy, or social justice?
Which of these three approaches is more permanent in its results?
Why is it important that the church be involved at all three levels in a time of rapid social change?

3. Education and poverty are closely related. This chapter talks about the work of United Methodists and our predecessor bodies in educational ministries, including the Sunday school and the work of The United Methodist Publishing House.

Ask: Beyond the Sunday school, in what educational ministries are we involved? (Support for colleges? Tutoring? Literacy programs?) What are the results of education in our community? Are graduates equipped to work and survive in today's economy? How many dropouts are there? Who is reaching out to them? In what ways can the church both support the work of the local school district and encourage it to become better than it is?

4. Ask: In what ways has the world progressed toward the vision of a peaceful humanity? (Note the work of the United Nations, nuclear disarmament, peacekeeping forces, efforts to eradicate disease, poverty, and illiteracy.)

If, as Wesley thought, war is "totally against all reason and common sense," why do we continue to spend so much time and money preparing for war?

5. Talk about Christian faith and racial/ethnic prejudice and oppression.

Ask: In our society, how do we tend to deal with persons of other races and/or ethnic groupings?

To be more specific, ask: How do we feel about issues such as affirmative action?

Do we cross the street rather than meet a group of persons of another race?

Do we associate issues such as poverty and crime with a particular ethnic group?

Remind the group that both the Scripture and the findings of modern scientific research teach us that we are, both literally and figuratively, siblings. The statement "God has made of one blood all peoples" is both a theological and a medical truth. Given that reality, what causes the hatreds and prejudices?

Ask the group to look at the record of United Methodists in working with persons of various races and cultures.

Ask: Are there persons of many races in our congregation? Why or why not?

Are there congregations in our community that minister to persons of specific races? (For example, an African Methodist Episcopal Church or a Korean United Methodist congregation?)

Consider inviting the pastor and/or some of the lay leadership from a congregation made up of another racial group than your own to meet with you and to explore some of the racial tensions felt within The United Methodist Church. Consider visiting one or more such congregations, not just to *look*, but to attempt to understand the importance of another cultural expression of the faith and to help ourselves be more open to persons who are different from us.

6. Close with prayer.

7

THE UNITED METHODIST CHURCH GOVERNMENT

If you are not familiar with the governmental structure of The United Methodist Church, consider inviting the pastor, your lay member of the annual conference, or another church leader to meet with you and to be a "consultant" for the session. *The Book of Discipline* would also be an important resource.

1. Begin by reminding the group of Wesley's gift for organization. Methodism first grew because he organized his converts into small groups called "classes." The members of these classes were responsible for one another's spiritual growth and Christian living. As the church grew, so did the organizational structure. The basic structure of the church has always been the "conference." In this session, we will talk about how the conference helps the church live its mission and ministry in the world.

2. At the local church level, there is the "charge conference." Ask your "consultant" to describe the work of the charge conference, both as the decision-making body in the local church and the catalyst for ministry.

3. The next "level" of government is the annual conference. United Methodists know about the annual conference primarily because of "apportionments" and "appointments." Ask your "consultant" to explain those two terms and how they relate the local church to the annual conference. Ask her or him also to describe how the annual conference empowers local churches to be in mission.

Ask: What conference agencies help resource and challenge the local church?

4. Then move to the General Conference, which is the only body that *speaks for* the entire denomination. Describe its function, or ask your consultant to do so. Talk about the importance of "speaking *for*" the church, as opposed to "speaking *to*" the church.

5. Tell the group that, so far, you have been talking about the "legislative branch" of the church government. We also have an "executive" and a "judicial" branch. The executive branch is composed of the Council of Bishops and the boards and agencies of the church. They are charged with carrying out the will of the General Conference. (Note that the executive branch cannot speak "for" the church but only "to" it.)

6. Finally, describe the work of the Judicial Council and its role in interpreting the consitutionality of conference legislation or rulings by the bishops. If there has been a meeting of the Judicial Council recently, there may be news items in the religious press that would illustrate the work of this body. (The Constitution of The United Methodist Church may be found on pages 21–38 of the *Book of Discipline*.)

7. After dealing with all questions, remind the group that the reason all three branches of the church exist is to make it possible for the local church to be in mission. Because we are "in connection" with all other United Methodist churches, we can more effectively be in mission worldwide.

8

UNITED METHODISM'S WORLD MISSION

Ahead of time, secure several maps of the world and/or globes. *National Geographic* maps are an excellent resource.

OR

Use the Peters Projection map that comes from the Children's Fund for Christian Mission. (Check with the local unit of United Methodist Women for maps.)

OR

The church may have a map showing the areas where United Methodist missions are happening.

You may also want to invite the coordinator of missions in your church to help lead this session.

1. Since this is the last session of the group, ask each person to answer the three questions one more time: Who am I? How am I? What do I bring to this session today?

2. Form several small teams. Give each team a map or globe. Point out the list of countries where there are United Methodist missions. Assign an area of the world to each team, for example, Europe.
   Ask each team to locate on the map the countries in their assigned area. (Note that some countries may only appear on the most recent maps or globes.)

Ask: What did you learn?

Which countries could you not find? Why?
What does this exercise suggest to us about the outreach of The United Methodist Church?

Remind the group of the difference between direct work, ecumenical cooperation, and partnerships.

3. Explain World Service and Advance Specials. **World Service** is the basic fund of the church. It pays for a variety of administrative expenses, including the staff expenses of the general boards and agencies and basic mission expenses (such as salaries of missionaries, and so on). It is, in a sense, the "price we pay" for being United Methodists. **Advance Specials** are opportunities for giving to specific causes, above and beyond World Service giving. Through Advance giving, we can designate money, for example, for salary support for a pastor in the Oklahoma Indian Mission Conference, a medical clinic in Tanzania, children's work in Latin America, and so on.

OR

You may want to ask your mission coordinator to explain these terms in relationship to the budget and the specific Advance Specials your congregation supports.

4. Talk about your congregation's specific involvement in mission. What do you do? If this is an energetic group, and there are adequate bulletin boards and other displays about mission in the church, have them do another "scavenger hunt," this time for ways your church is in mission beyond the community where you live. Our congregation, for example, is helping pay for a church building for a new Methodist congregation in Bulgaria and helping support two students in the Baltic Seminary, as well as contributing to Mountain Top, a service/mission project in the Cumberland Plateau. In addition, United Methodist Men, United Methodist Women, and United Methodist Youth are involved in support for other mission projects.

Talk about ways individuals and families can be involved in mission to the entire world.

5. Close with a prayer of thanksgiving for the time your group has had together and for guidance for the future.